William P. Roberts

M A R R I A G E

Sacrament of Hope and Challenge

D1601596

IF GOD loved us so much,
we too should love each other.
1 John 4:11

To my wife Challon
with much love

Nihil Obstat: Rev. Thomas Richstatter, O.F.M.
           Rev. Robert L. Hagedorn

Imprimi Potest: Rev. Jeremy Harrington, O.F.M.
           Provincial

Imprimatur: +James H. Garland, V.G.
           Archdiocese of Cincinnati
           July 11, 1988

Book design and cover by Julie Lonneman.

ISBN 0-86716-102-7

Foreword

*T*his new edition of *Marriage: Sacrament of Hope and Challenge* has an even more personal dimension: It invites couples to strengthen their own marriages by intimate discussion and shared prayer. To this end, this volume contains four additions to the original text:

1) An appropriate Scripture text at the beginning of each chapter provides the biblical ground for the chapter's content and a basis for prayer.

2) A Partner-to-Partner Inventory at the end of each chapter invites couples to assess the strengths and weaknesses of their own marriages in the context of the chapter discussion. (The questions included in the original text, designed for individual or classroom use, have been retained with some minor editing.)

3) So that this book may be integrated into a couple's prayer life, each chapter closes with a Prayer Service. These Prayer Services, designed for use either by an individual couple or by a group of couples, reflect the chapter's major themes and are based on the key Scripture texts. Pray-ers should feel free to adapt these services to their own particular tastes and needs.

4) A new chapter on the family as domestic Church stresses

iii

practical ways of growing in family unity.

My hope is that this new edition will enrich the relationships of married couples as well as provide insights into the mystery of marriage for all its readers.

Finally, I wish to thank Carol Luebering, editor at St. Anthony Messenger Press, for inviting me to produce this revised version of *Marriage: Sacrament of Hope and Challenge*.

CONTENTS

CONTENTS

Introduction

Introduction

Marriage! The word evokes many diverse images and memories: love and unity, hatred and bitterness; tenderness and understanding, harshness and misinterpretation; hopes and dreams, disappointments and failures; peace and joy, strain and heartbreak; trust and fidelity, fear and broken promises; music and dance, cursing and fighting. No wonder we are attracted by marriage's promise of growth and happiness and, at the same time, fearful of its destructive potential.

Neither romanticism nor crippling fear is a proper response to the different realities that marriage in today's world involves. Marriage is not something that happens to us. It is a reality that we make happen. We make the choices that shape the quality and meaning marriage will hold for us.

The conviction that the responsibility for molding a marriage lies squarely on human shoulders is the impetus behind the writing of this book.

For the Christian, faith can give light and strength, guidance and courage in the lifelong task of creating and sustaining a marriage. Faith, however, is not magic. It never operates automatically. Married couples must live out their commitment to

Christ in terms of the practical concrete challenges of daily relationship: attitude and word, body language and action. The present book is offered as a contribution to this life-giving enterprise.

The book takes as its central theme an insight that is almost as old as Christianity itself: that marriage between two Christians is a sacrament or sign of the love between Christ and his people. But what does this mean in concrete terms? What does it imply for the kind of marriage two Christians should be striving to create day by day? What type of ongoing relationship with Christ does it presuppose on the part of the couple? What practical difference can it make for a richer, more mutually satisfying marital relationship between two adults? These are some of the questions that will be addressed in exploring the sacramentality of Christian marriage.

To accomplish this task, we will first look at the biblical foundation of our Christian understanding of marriage. The sacramentality of Christian marriage will then be further viewed in relationship to several central themes of Christian faith: the reign of God, ministry, death and resurrection, the Eucharist. Throughout the book the main thrust will be to apply this sacramental understanding of Christian marriage to the practical realities of daily life.

This book is not intended as a complete treatise on marriage. There is no such thing. It is meant, rather, to set forth clearly the Christian underpinnings of current insights into marriage and to point to some of the implications these have for a meaningful marital relationship. In this way it strives to underscore the Christian dimension of married life and to foster its enrichment.

In determining the scope of this book, two decisions were made that deserve some explanation:

First, in deciding to focus on the *sacramental* aspects of Christian marriage, a treatment of *ethical* questions (such as birth control, abortion and remarriage after divorce) has intentionally been omitted. These issues, important though they be, continue to receive more than ample coverage in journals, books and the mass media. I would not wish their inclusion here to distract from the central purpose of this book.

Second, because this book is primarily for the vast majority of Christians who are either already married or preparing for marriage rather than for theologians and canon lawyers, a nontechnical style has been chosen and footnotes omitted.

Besides being written for a general reading public, this book is intended for use in college and senior high school marriage courses and in marriage preparation and enrichment programs. In such settings, a book by a psychologist or marriage counselor that addresses daily problems and difficulties in more detail would be a helpful adjunct.

To facilitate the application of the theological insights in this book, questions for reflection and discussion follow each chapter.

I present this book on Christian marriage at a time when many people are seriously questioning the relevance of both Christianity and marriage. My efforts will be fruitful if it helps enkindle renewed hope in married life that, in turn, inspires more generous response from married Christians to the challenge of building a permanent relationship in authentic and mutually satisfying love.

YAHWEH GOD SAID, "It is not right that the man should be alone. I shall make him a helper. So from the soil Yahweh God fashioned all the wild animals and all the birds of heaven. These he brought to the man to see what he would call them; each one was to bear the name the man would give it. The man gave names to all the cattle, all the birds of heaven and all the wild animals. But no helper suitable for the man was found for him. Then, Yahweh God made the man fall into a deep sleep. And, while he was asleep, he took one of his ribs and closed the flesh up again forthwith. Yahweh God fashioned the rib he had taken from the man into a woman, and brought her to the man. And the man said:

> This one at last is bone of my bones
>   and flesh of my flesh!
> She is to be called Woman,
>   because she was taken from Man.

This is why a man leaves his father and mother and becomes attached to his wife, and they become one flesh.

Now, both of them were naked, the man and his wife, but they felt no shame before each other.

(Genesis 2:4b-7, 18-25)

ONE

Becoming One Body

A vast variety of relationships constitutes the fabric of human life: parents and children, close friends and casual acquaintances, professional colleagues and business associates, jogging partners and fellow weight-watchers. Diverse as these relationships are in terms of intimacy, none claim the kind of oneness that ought to exist between wife and husband. Only marriage is designed to constitute two people as truly one.

This oneness is not achieved automatically or overnight. It is a lifelong process in which two persons gradually live out their commitment to become one body.

This concept of becoming one flesh is unique and fundamental to marriage. It will therefore be probed at some length before we reflect on the dimensions of marital union that are specifically related to faith in Jesus Christ.

One Body

The Bible begins with two accounts of creation which differ in detail but not in issue. Both emphasize humanity's role in God's plan.

The first (Genesis 1:1—2:4a) presents humanity as the culmination of creation, God's finishing touch to a world already teeming with life. The second (Genesis 2:4b-25) places the creation of the first man before all other forms of life, the key element in God's plan for the world's fruitfulness. This second account speaks of human loneliness and of the Creator's compassionate attempts to provide a suitable partner for this creature—domestic and wild animals, the birds of the air. The story ends with the formation of the first woman from the man's rib, and the fundamental Judeo-Christian theological statement about marriage:

> That is why a man leaves his father and mother and clings
> to his wife, and the two of them become one body.
> (Genesis 2:24, NAB)

To understand the phrase, "becoming one body," it is first necessary to understand what the ancient Hebrews meant by the word *body*. Unlike the Greeks, who had a dualistic body-soul view of a human being, the Hebrews perceived a person in a holistic way. In biblical thought, the human was seen not as composed of two separate entities, a body and a soul, but rather as one whole: embodied spirit, inspirited flesh. Accordingly, when the creation account speaks of woman and man becoming one body, it is not speaking of mere physical unity. The oneness that is meant to take place in marriage is the coming together of two whole persons. Marriage is the call and the challenge to two people to become united in mind and heart, in body and in spirit.

We can consider two different couples:

The first are physically attracted to each other and have a very active, physically satisfying sex life. Beyond that, they have little else in common. They are unable to discuss their thoughts and feelings; they enjoy no common hobbies and are not involved in what is really going on in each other's lives. They are "one" only in a physical way. This physical closeness is not a sign of a fulfilling personal union. It cloaks, at least for a time, serious areas of estrangement. They are not one in the biblical sense.

6

The second couple are very attracted to the way each other thinks, to each other's sensitivity, to the religious and moral ideals that they share. They enjoy doing many things together and like to discuss the hobbies each pursues alone. Both are interested in and concerned about what is happening within the other. Their sexual expression of love is very fulfilling in terms of frequency and physical passion. More importantly, it expresses the many levels of sharing that bind them together. This couple is becoming one.

Becoming: A Process

The word *becoming* in the phrase "becoming one body" underscores the *process* dimension in marriage. Too often people think of marriage as if it were a once-and-for-all event completed on the wedding day. But the wedding day only marks the beginning of a dynamic new reality. The relationship that has already grown between two people prior to marriage undergoes an essential transformation when the two commit themselves to live out their lives in marital union. They vow permanent commitment, not an entrance into a static way of life. They promise to embark together on the process of becoming one enfleshed spirit—a process never completed before the journey together in this life ends.

The wedding day *is* a definitive occasion in one sense: It marks a decisive step into a radically different kind of relationship. From that day two people have a new responsibility for one another. They have wedded themselves together in a unique bond. Yet, in another sense, they will never completely achieve unity. The two are committed and challenged to risk becoming more married every day. Indeed, the two become "married" according to the degree of oneness they achieve.

A couple who view marriage as a once-and-for-all event completed on the wedding day limit themselves to living out of the past instead of creating a new present and a new future. "We are married, so now we are stuck with each other." "We are married, so now *you* have these duties and obligations." "We are married, so now it is no longer necessary to 'court,' to be seductive, to create new moments of surprise, excitement and wonder for one another."

An entirely different picture emerges when we enter marriage as an adventure. An adventure is open-ended. The success of this adventure depends on a firm commitment to grow in support, trust and love of each other. We create our path and discover our way as we go. Though there are risks, we are moved by a sense of excitement and expectation. While there might be unforeseen pitfalls and obstacles, we have the power to create new discoveries and surprises, new levels of joy and satisfaction. The adventure is never over until death causes physical separation.

Oneness

Finally, we must understand the meaning of the word *one* in our perception of marriage as "becoming one body." The unity spoken of here is not a merging of two personalities into one. The sacrifice of precious individuality does not make a loving union.

Nor does this union result from the domination of one person by another. A relationship in which the opinions, decisions and desires of one person are controlled by the other is less than life-sustaining. Authentic marital union demands that neither person's freedom be impaired by the other. The response to the will of another that promotes genuine oneness in marriage must be made with free, self-determined love, and not because of fear of one's spouse or fear of one's inner self.

Two people achieve real oneness in marriage when they become increasingly present to each other as gift in love. In this way they enter into one another. They dwell in each other. They become a part of one another. They think and care about each other more and more. Their lives, hopes and destinies become increasingly intertwined. Deep empathy develops between them.

At the same time, this belonging to each other must leave both of them *other*. Each must remain beyond the total comprehension, possession and grasp of the other. They must ever be two unrepeatably unique individuals, each of whom grows in her or his uniqueness and independent self-esteem, in the context of a deepening relationship.

In each person there is always a dimension of mystery, a dimension of being which eludes all concepts, analysis and classification. Even to oneself a person remains a mystery. In marital love two people share the mystery of themselves and grow in the love and respect of that mystery.

A Revolutionary Concept

Having probed the term "becoming one body," it is appropriate to ask about its significance first in the context of the ancient world, and then in modern society.

The Genesis creation account (Genesis 2:4b-25) in which the notion appears was put in written form about the 10th century B.C.E., quite probably by a member of David's royal court. At that time in the ancient Near East, polygamy was an acceptable way of life, and infidelity on the part of the male spouse was tolerated. The wife, on the other hand, was bound to one husband; she was literally his property.

Against this cultural background, the biblical author proclaims a revolutionary thought: that a man "leaves his father and mother and *clings* to his wife, and the two of them become *one* body" (Genesis 2:24, NAB; emphasis added).

Twenty-nine centuries of repetition have made this biblical passage a commonplace in human life; yet it is not clear how seriously it is really being taken even today. While American society long ago ruled polygamy illegal, "serial marriage" has become an acceptable and almost expected way of life. A sizable number of marriages that do last do so only as convenient arrangements or as pacts of peaceful coexistence. Many aspects of American life—the tax structure, the climbing of the corporate ladder—militate against married life and obstruct the nurture of marital union.

In this contemporary context, what can one say? Is Genesis 2:24 a relic from an ancient age, without any relevance for today's civilized and sophisticated society? Or is the call to wife and husband to become one a prophetic challenge that might save us from widespread breakdown in interpersonal relationships and lead us to enriched lives of fidelity and love? My belief is that the latter is true.

Oneness and Equality

An essential condition for wife and husband to become one is acceptance of the fact that woman and man are equal. The Book of Genesis provides significant insights into this equality.

The first creation account presents man and woman as equals, twin aspects of one reality:

> God created man in the image of himself,
> in the image of God he created him,
> male and female he created them. (Genesis 1:27)

The same idea is evident in a later passage:

> On the day that God created Adam he made him in the likeness of God. Male and female he created them. He blessed them and gave them the name Man, when they were created. (Genesis 5:1-2)

The oneness in marriage described in the second creation account is rooted in the very creation of our race:

> Yahweh God said, "It is not right that the man should be alone. I shall make him a helper." So from the soil Yahweh God fashioned all the wild animals and all the birds of heaven. These he brought to the man to see what he would call them; each one was to bear the name the man would give it. The man gave names to all the cattle, all the birds of heaven and all the wild animals. But no helper suitable for the man was found for him. Then, Yahweh God made the man fall into a deep sleep. And, while he was asleep, he took one of his ribs and closed the flesh up again forthwith. Yahweh God fashioned the

rib he had taken from the man into a woman, and
brought her to the man. And the man said:

> This one at last is bone of my bones
> and flesh of my flesh!
> She is to be called Woman,
> because she was taken from Man. (Genesis 2:18-23)

The creation of humanity was incomplete without woman.
The male found none of the animals to be his equal; only the
woman is a suitable companion. She alone is bone of his bones,
flesh of his flesh. She is his alter ego, indeed, one of his ribs. The
significance of the word *rib* is heightened when it is recalled that
Arabic people still refer to a bosom friend as their "rib."

Even the terms *help, helper* and *helpmate* which refer to
woman in many translations of Genesis 2:18, though they
connote inferiority in our culture, had a distinctly personal
meaning in the Old Testament. When the psalmist calls God "our
help" (Psalm 33:20), the term means refuge or support, the staff
upon which we can lean, the one in whom we can trust and in
whom we can find security. In that sense, the term *helper* contains
no hint of inequality.

Equality does not mean sameness. Equality in no way
obscures the obvious sexual differences between female and male.
Nor does it cloud over the real diversities that exist between any
wife and husband in the area of gifts, capabilities and
responsibilities. These diversities, however, cannot be stereotyped
according to sex.

What constitutes the basic equality of persons is the radical
human potential for intelligence, love and free self-
determination—precisely what differentiates humans from all
other creatures. In marriage two persons share that which makes
them equal as humans: their minds, their hearts, their free choice
to become one with each other.

Because wife and husband are equal as persons, they have
equal responsibility in bringing about oneness in their marriage.
The wife and husband together are coheads, cofounders,
coauthors of the marital community. Together they bring it into

11

being. The free decisions that each of them makes in regard to the marriage form it into the particular reality it becomes.

The dynamic of this ongoing process of creating a marriage does not require that one person takes most of the initiative and makes all the decisions while the other responds and obeys. Rather, it consists in two adults communicating to each other the best of what is on their minds and in their hearts. Both must listen and respond to each other in truth, trust and love, and make decisions accordingly. The wife and husband jointly constitute the authority in the marital relationship. They share final decision-making power in matters that affect living and growing together in oneness.

There are different ways in which a couple can exercise their joint authority. In major decisions (buying a house, choosing a neighborhood to live in or a school for the children) both spouses will be fully engaged in the decision-making process. Basic agreement is necessary before they make a final decision. At other times spouses exercise joint authority by agreeing that one of them will handle most of the decision-making in a particular area (making up the menus, caring for the garden or keeping the car in running condition).

The Opposing View

This concept of joint authority stands in contrast to a long-standing cultural view. Despite the feminist consciousness-raising that has taken place in western culture in recent years, male domination in marriage finds vigorous defense in many fundamentalist circles, in some quarters of the charismatic movement and within the opposition to the Equal Rights Amendment. Since these groups claim biblical support for their views, they cannot be ignored in a theological discussion of marriage. The biblical imagery that serves as a basis of their perspective is drawn from Genesis 2:18-24 and 3:16, and from Ephesians 5 (which will be treated in the next chapter).

Genesis 2:18-24, cited above as calling for equality and unity, has also been interpreted as giving biblical support to male supremacy in marriage because the male is portrayed as being created first, while the female is taken from him. Such interpretation misses the point.

As contemporary biblical scholarship makes clear, the creation account is not a historical or scientific explanation of how humanity was actually created. It is, rather, a theological statement that God is the creator of humanity and intended that woman and man become one flesh in marriage. This faith insight stands in opposition not only to the sacred prostitution rites current at the time this passage was written, but also to polygamy and adultery. In a culture where a wife was property, the creation of the male prior to the female is hardly startling and has no theological significance. Of real import are the theological insights about the unity and equality between wife and husband that logically lead to a condemnation of all infidelity and inequality in marriage.

On the surface, Genesis 3:16 seems to pose a greater problem for equality of spouses. In that verse God says to Eve:

> I shall give you intense pain in childbearing,
> you will give birth to your children in pain.
> Your yearning will be for your husband,
> and he will dominate you. (Genesis 3:16)

Doesn't this end the debate once and for all, and prove beyond a shadow of a doubt that God's everlasting will for a wife is that she be under the rule of her husband? Quite the contrary!

The first two chapters in the Book of Genesis treat of creation and God's original intent for humanity. Chapter 3, on the other hand, is concerned with sin and its consequences in human life. After sinning, Adam points the finger of accusation at Eve (see Genesis 3:12). *Because of human sin* the husband, who had been called to become one flesh with his wife, lords it over her instead. Genesis 3:16 does *not* proclaim God's will for spouses. It rather describes the sad condition of marriage that resulted from human violation of God's will.

The view that God does not wish any human to dominate or

"lord it over" another is supported in the New Testament by Christ's teaching on authority. Jesus contrasts the pagan practice of "lording it over" others with the Christian ideal:

> You know that among the gentiles the rulers lord it over them, and great men make their authority felt. Among you this is not to happen. No; anyone who wants to become great among you must be your servant, and anyone who wants to be first among you must be your slave, just as the Son of man came not to be served but to serve, and to give his life as a ransom for many.
>
> (Matthew 20:25b-28)

Practical Implications

The concept of becoming one is a beautiful ideal. But how, in reality, can two people work together toward its achievement? There are obviously no complete answers to this question. Some important points, however, can be indicated:

1) *The couple's behavior toward each other must foster unity rather than disunity.* Unity doesn't just happen. A couple must work to build a close relationship. One way they do this is by showing each other respect and appreciation. They do not take each other for granted. They avoid bickering, nagging and cutting each other down. They make an effort to say "thank you." They praise one another even for modest accomplishments: the tasty chocolate cake, the freshly cut lawn, patience with a restless child.

2) *A couple must work toward oneness within the limitations of their own marriage.* There is no such thing as a "dream marriage." Marriages do not exist in dreams, but in the reality of two limited human beings, working with limited amounts of energy and ability to build what can be only an imperfect marital bond. A couple must work toward a realistic acceptance of the inborn limitations of their marital relationship. At the same time they must strive to bring to birth the yet untapped potential that their marriage has for greater union and happiness.

Two extremes need to be avoided: complacency and unrealistic expectation.

14

A complacent couple make little effort to improve their communication or their mutual sexual satisfaction. They let day-to-day boredom settle into their marriage. They passively put up with nagging faults: sloppiness, sarcasm, insensitivity. "What can we do about it anyway?" "Neither of us will ever change, so why try?"

The other extreme is a couple looking for a storybook marriage, "living happily ever after." They envision a marriage without harsh words, misunderstandings or fights. They dream of a marriage where all meals are delicious and peaceful, where every sexual expression of love reaches the heights.

The art of marriage involves walking between the extremes of complacency, on the one hand, and daydreaming about the impossible, on the other. The prayer of Alcoholics Anonymous is applicable to every marriage:

> God grant me the serenity to accept the things
> I cannot change,
> courage to change the things I can,
> and wisdom to know the difference.

3) *Since each person is uniquely individual, the "one" that each married couple strive to become is unique.* No two marriages are identical. One's expectations of marriage should not be rigidly based on any other marriage, including that of one's parents or one's best friend.

Each marriage reaches its own quality of union and finds its own particular mode of expression. Such matters as roles and functions, ways of relating to one another and the size of the family must be shaped by each unique couple.

It is tempting to impose on a spouse an idyllic picture of one's mother or father and then expect the spouse to measure up. Some demand that their marriage be every bit as good as they thought their parents' marriage was—or should have been. A person may feel the pressure to have children as early in marriage as an older sibling did, or to stay home all day tending the house as grandmother did.

Each couple must decide what their marriage will be in light

15

of *their* individual personalities, interests and aspirations. What works in one marriage will not work in exactly the same way in another. Models, suggestions and advice must be carefully considered, not blindly followed.

4) *Becoming one in marriage requires mature response to ongoing change.* Every human life is, of its nature, an evolutionary process. Accordingly, marriage is the coming together of two people who are growing and changing in a relationship which must also grow and change. In *Passages* Gail Sheehy describes the stages of adult development: the 20's, when one learns to take hold in the adult world; turning 30, when discontent and a desire to broaden one's horizons set in, the "Dead-line Decade" between 35 and 45; and a time of new stability around the mid-40's. To these can be added the period of transition to late adulthood and late adulthood itself. A couple need to understand and accept the states of ordinary adult development so that they may better cope with the crises that each stage presents.

Besides the changes necessarily linked with human growth, other events can dramatically affect the marriage and alter its course. Children, professional promotions and demotions, loss of job and residential moves demand varying degrees of adjustments. The birth of an exceptional infant, disability, serious illness or the death of a child can test a marriage to its limits.

Change never leaves a relationship untouched. In its wake a married couple will either drift further apart or continue to draw closer with renewed determination and rekindled hope. The more a couple can meet changing circumstances in a spirit of love, trust and open communication with each other, the better chance they have of growing in oneness through the crisis.

5) *The married couple must be faithful to the commitment to become one.* Too often marital fidelity is spoken of primarily in the negative sense: "You shall not commit adultery." Marital fidelity, however, demands much more. Being faithful to each other means being full of faith *in* each other. It means to trust and love each other, to believe in the other's worth and in the future of the relationship. Marital fidelity is a continuing choice to give life to

another and to accept the gift of life in return. It is to walk hand in hand into the future, not knowing what strange winds might blow, but believing that nothing can destroy the bond of love.

The question, then, is not only whether some*one* else has come between a couple. It also must be whether some*thing* else has come between them: the job, TV, a career, the children, apathy, boredom!

The question of fidelity must also center around what husband and wife positively contribute to each other and to the blossoming of their marriage. How much energy and imagination go into finding ways to endear themselves to one another? How faithful are they to all the little attentions: the midday phone call, the love note tucked into the lunch bag or left on the pillow, the single rose on the breakfast table? How much do they seek each other's companionship—an all-day picnic, a short evening walk, or a late dinner for two?

To be in love is to be fully alive in the presence of another. To be faithful is to enkindle that love and nourish forever that life.

6) *The couple must own the responsibility for their marriage, not shift responsibility to God.* Despite the old saying, marriages are *not* made in heaven. They are made on earth. They are created by two people who bind themselves together in marital union. While each couple has a unique relationship with God, a unique call from God, it is *their* response to God's grace that gives their marriage its unique shape.

The failings that occur in marriage and societal obstacles that put added strain on married life are not God's fault. Adultery, drunkenness, physical and verbal abuse, addiction to work and lack of consideration are of human origin. Humans create the circumstances that put undue stress on a marriage: tax penalties, inadequate wage scales, pressure to climb the promotional ladder. Only humans, in openness to God's help and to each other, can correct the conditions that adversely affect married life.

Destructive relationships and unfulfilled marriages cannot be attributed to the will of God. God's will is love, and the peace and joy that flow from love. The barriers to discovering this union are

17

not to be found in God but in ourselves.

This is not to say, however, that humans are always blameworthy when a marriage falls short of the ideal or even breaks down. Human responsibility is not synonymous with human culpability.

7) *Communication and growth in marital oneness are interdependent.* The ability to communicate one's deepest thoughts and feelings to one's spouse presumes a certain degree of unity already achieved. On the other hand, unity continues to grow only through meaningful, ongoing communication.

Any couple serious about enriching their marriage must be committed to regular personal communication as a priority. They must create opportunities when they can be alone together and engage in real conversation—over lunch, for a half hour after dinner, after the children have gone to bed. They need to talk about the joys and difficulties in their own marriage, in their jobs, in their relationships with others. They grow closer by sharing music and art, what they are reading, how they feel about what is going on in the political world. In short, each lives a life worth talking about and shares those experiences that stimulate interest.

A couple must also be concerned about ever improving their communication skills. Reading an occasional article on the topic, attending a communication workshop or a marriage encounter weekend are just some of the ways in which a couple might grow in the art of communication.

Even when a marital relationship has been badly damaged, the admission that there is a communication problem might well be the first step toward a healing. When such a couple decide to seek help in acquiring better communication skills, they are already on the road toward marital growth.

Conclusion

The biblical insight into marriage as a process in which two people become one flesh is the foundation of our theological understanding of marriage. Having probed this concept and

18

explored some of its practical implications, we will next consider how this perception of marriage is enriched by relationship with Jesus Christ.

For Reflection or Discussion

1) The author says that marital unity is based on mutual respect for the individuality of each partner. Are there any ways in which the differences between two persons can actually contribute to greater unity of mind and purpose?

2) What convictions do you hold about equality between the sexes?

3) What qualities do you associate with an ideal marriage? What marriages have you observed which closely resemble your ideal? What personal attributes or attitudes in yourself present obstacles to achieving that ideal? Which bring the ideal within reach?

4) When was the last time you were able to communicate your deepest feelings to another person? What factors made it possible for you to communicate on that level? What obstacles did you have to overcome?

Partner-to-Partner Inventory

1) To what extent do we experience respect, appreciation, courtesy and sensitivity in our relationship? To what degree is there bickering, nagging or cutting remarks?

2) Have we become complacent in our relationship? In what ways does this complacency manifest itself? What unrealistic expectations about a "dream marriage" do we continue to entertain?

3) How free are we to create the uniqueness of our own relationship? Or are we under pressure—either internally or externally—to shape our relationship according to some other model? Explain.

4) During the course of our relationship, have notable changes taken place in our lives? In what ways has our relationship grown stronger through these changes? In what ways have we grown apart?

5) What are the ways in which we have experienced faithfulness from one another in our relationship? Are there any ways in which we have experienced unfaithfulness? What are our hopes and fears in regard to faithfulness in the future of our relationship?

6) In what ways are we satisfied with the level of communication we have thus far achieved? What present limitations and obstacles do we continue to experience in our efforts to communicate? Do we have practical suggestions for overcoming the limits and for improving the intimacy of our communication?

7) In our view, is the husband the head of the house and the ultimate authority over his wife? Or do we see wife and husband as coauthors of the family community? Whom do we perceive as the final decision-maker in the marriage? On what basis do we think functions and chores in the family are to be assigned: on the basis of gender stereotypes or on the basis of personal interests, talents and availability?

PRAYER SERVICE

Becoming One

Opening Prayer

God, you are one: Father, Word and Spirit. You have made us to
your image and likeness. You have called us to this marriage so
that we may reflect your oneness in our personal union with each
other. As we thank you for the oneness we already enjoy, we
rededicate ourselves to our commitment to become increasingly
united in truth and love. Amen.

Scripture Reading

> I pray not only for these
> but also for those
> who through their teaching will come to believe in me.
> May they all be one,
> just as, Father, you are in me and I am in you,
> so that they also may be in us,
> so that the world may believe it was you who sent me.
> I have given them the glory you gave to me,
> that they may be one as we are one.
> With me in them and you in me,
> may they be so perfected in unity
> that the world will recognize that it was you who sent me
> and that you have loved them as you loved me.
>
> (John 17:20-23)

Silent reflection

Sharing of thoughts on the reading

Litany

This Litany reflects three different moods: thanksgiving, penitence and resolution. Couples should pause between the sections and allow themselves to settle into the mood of the prayer.

For our marriage,
> We thank you, Lord.

For the joy of our union,
> We thank you, Lord.

For our fidelity and love,
> We thank you, Lord.

For the intimacy we have achieved,
> We thank you, Lord.

For the ways we have blocked communication,
> Lord have mercy.

For the times we have closed ourselves to intimacy,
> Lord have mercy.

For the occasions when we lacked respect
for each other's dignity and uniqueness,
> Lord have mercy.

For any infidelity to our commitment to grow in love
for one another,
> Lord, have mercy.

We will strive to show greater sensitivity
toward each other's feelings,
> Lord, help us, we pray.

We will make an effort to listen and respond
to each other's yearnings,
> Lord, help us, we pray.

We will do the following things to bring about
greater intimacy between us:
  (The couple share these.)
  Lord, help us, we pray.

*If they wish, the couple may renew their exchange of rings as a sign
of their continued commitment.*

Concluding Prayer
(Recite together.)

I shall sing the faithful love of Yahweh forever,
from age to age my lips shall declare your constancy,
for you have said: love is built to last for ever,
you have fixed your constancy firm in the heavens.

The heavens praise your wonders, Yahweh,
Your constancy in the gathering of your faithful.
Who in the skies can compare with Yahweh?
Who among the sons of god can rival him?

How blessed the nation that learns to acclaim you!
They will live, Yahweh, in the light of your presence.
  In your name they rejoice all day long,
    by your saving justice they are raised up.

I shall sing the faithful love of Yahweh for ever,
from age to age my lips shall declare your constancy,
for you have said: love is built to last for ever,
you have fixed your constancy firm in the heavens.

(Psalm 89:1-2, 5-6, 15-16)

Kiss of Peace

I GIVE YOU a new commandment:
love one another;
you must love one another
just as I have loved you.
It is by your love for one another,
that everyone will recognize you
as my disciples. (John 13:34-35)

A Sign of Christ's Love

*P*eople experience marriage in disparate ways. Affection, concern and acceptance characterize many marital relationships. Coldness, indifference and petty criticism mar others. Some couples enjoy extraordinary degrees of generosity, gentleness and intimate communion. Others destroy one another with self-centeredness, cruelty and hatred.

Clearly, not every marriage reflects the goodness of God and the love of Christ. Only through their growing dedication to each other do couples discover the intimate connection between married love and Christ's love.

In this chapter we explore what it means to call Christian marriage a sacrament, and the implications that this has for both the life of faith and the experience of marriage.

Old Testament Roots

The seeds for the later understanding of marriage as a sacrament were already planted in the prophetic writings. One of the ways in which the prophets described God's love was in the imagery of marriage. The prophet Hosea, for instance, saw in his own wife's infidelity Israel's repeated rejection of Yahweh. A startling insight into God's love enabled him to remain faithful and forgiving until reconciliation was won. Hosea drew from his own experience an inspired song of God's fidelity:

> I shall betroth you to myself for ever,
> I shall betroth you in uprightness and justice,
> and faithful love and tenderness.
> Yes, I shall betroth you to myself in loyalty
> and in the knowledge of Yahweh. (Hosea 2:21-22)

About two centuries later, during the Babylonian Exile, the Isaian prophet expressed God's love for Israel in similar fashion.

> Do not fear, you will not be put to shame again,
> do not worry, you will not be disgraced again;
> for you will forget the shame of your youth
> and no longer remember the dishonor of your
>   widowhood.
> For your Creator is your husband,
> Yahweh Sabaoth is his name,
> the Holy One of Israel is your redeemer,
> he is called God of the whole world.
> Yes, Yahweh has called you back
> like a forsaken, grief-stricken wife,
> like the repudiated wife of his youth,
> says your God.
>
> For the mountains may go away
> and the hills may totter,
> but my faithful love will never leave you,
> my covenant of peace will never totter,
> says Yahweh who takes pity on you. (Isaiah 54:4-6, 10)

New Testament Insights

In the New Testament Christ is perceived as creating a new covenant, a new bond of love between God and humans. Through the love Jesus manifests in his ministry and in his death and resurrection, he shows how much God loves us.

In light of our belief in the love of Jesus Christ, marriage takes on a new meaning. The human experience of marital commitment becomes for us Christians a visible, tangible path to deeper perception into Christ's love. We cannot see Christ. We cannot tangibly measure his love. We do, however, see married people who very much love and care for one another. They live for each other. They are willing to die for one another. Their unique love reflects Christ's total self-giving to his people and the people's response to Christ.

The text that serves as a foundation for the Christian understanding of marriage as a sign or sacrament of Christ's love comes from the Letter to the Ephesians. It stands at the beginning of a section that constitutes a household code. The author tells members of a household how they should relate to each other as Christians. He treats, in turn, those relationships that constituted a household at the time: wife-husband, child-parent, slave-master. It is in this context that his famous passage on marriage appears.

> Be subject to one another out of reverence for Christ. Wives should be subject to their husbands as to the Lord, since, as Christ is head of the Church and saves the whole body, so is a husband the head of his wife; and as the Church is subject to Christ, so should wives be to their husbands, in everything. Husbands should love their wives, just as Christ loved the Church and sacrificed himself for her to make her holy by washing her in cleansing water with a form of words, so that when he took the Church to himself she would be glorious, with no speck or wrinkle or anything like that, but holy and faultless. In the same way, husbands must love their wives as they love their own bodies; for a man to love his wife is for him to love himself. A man never hates his own body, but he feeds it and looks after it; and that is the way Christ treats the Church, because we are parts of his Body. This is why a man leaves his father and mother and becomes attached to his wife, and the two become one flesh. This mystery has great significance, but I am applying it to Christ and the Church. To sum up: you also, each one of you, must love his wife as he loves himself; and let every wife respect her husband.
>
> (Ephesians 5:21-33)

Many people hear in this passage only the mandate of wifely submission. But we must not allow the central insight into the link between marital love and Christ's love to escape us. The framework of marriage that was imbedded in first-century culture is necessarily reflected in this passage. Woven into that cultural framework were several presuppositions: that women were inferior to men; that the husband was, therefore, head of his wife who was to be submissive to him in all things; that men were capable of love while women, being inferior beings, were unable to love but only to respect and obey. These presuppositions and the framework of marriage built on them do not originate in the Letter to the Ephesians. Rather, this concept of marriage appears in the epistle because it was the marital framework the author— and his audience—knew from experience. Hence, it was the model into which he could weave his Christian insights.

What the Pauline author does is to view the culture-bound marital structure in the light of Christ's relationship with us. This light reveals significant insights that transform the marriage relationship even in a culture where the male is deemed superior.

1) He exhorts all Christians to "be subject to one another out of reverence for Christ." The call to mutual deference provides the leading thought on which the rest of the text is based.

2) The author draws a comparison between Christ's role and that of a husband. As "Christ is head of the Church and saves the whole body, so is a husband head of his wife." In other words, the manner in which Christ is head of the Church serves as the model for the way in which the husband should be head of his wife. And how is Christ head of the Church? The author immediately brings this critical question into focus. Christ is the head who gave himself fully and freely to bring to life a new creation: the Church.

In the preceding chapter, we recalled that Christ made a clear distinction between the way the pagans "lorded it" over others and the way Christians should exercise authority. Christ is Lord—and head of the Church—but he does not "lord it" over others. He has become servant of all, even unto death on the cross (see Matthew 20:25-28; Philippians 2:6-11).

Even in a cultural framework which perceives the husband as head of the wife, the husband must manifest this headship as Christ does. This means he cannot exercise control over his wife by giving high-handed orders, by making unreasonable demands, or by expecting his wife to be the servant who caters to all his self-centered whims. This Pauline text prohibits the husband from putting pressure on his wife to do things that go against her conscience or that violate her dignity, freedom or self-respect.

According to the author, there is only one way in which a Christian husband can exercise authority. Husbands must love and sacrifice themselves for their wives and have a sanctifying effect on them, "just as Christ loved the Church and sacrificed himself for her to make her holy." Husbands exercise authority by loving their wives "as they love their own bodies." A man does not hate his own body, but nourishes it and cares for it. So too must a man love, nourish and look after his wife as Christ cares for us, the living members of his body, the Church.

3) The author says that wives should respond to their husbands as the Church responds to Christ. The presupposition for this response is the wife's experience of her husband's Christlike love. Since Christ gives of himself totally to his people, they in turn are called to respond to him without reserve. In this way they enter into oneness with Christ. In a similar manner, a wife is to respond to the Christlike love of her husband.

To interpret the Pauline author as demanding a wife to respond in obedience to her husband outside the context of love would be a great distortion of the text. What he is calling for is openness to love, not to hatred; to sacrifice, not to exploitation; to a healing touch, not to violent abuse.

A Nonsexist Approach

The author of the Letter to the Ephesians could not be expected to break entirely out of his culture and its understanding of marriage. He did, however, plant the theological seeds that

29

point to a radically new experience of marriage which can ultimately lead to a model of true equality between wife and husband.

The task of freeing the theology of Ephesians from its male-dominated imagery is eased when the passage is read in the context of other important Pauline insights:

> But now that faith has come we are no longer under a slave looking after us; for all of you are the children of God, through faith, in Christ Jesus, since every one of you that has been baptized has been clothed in Christ. There can be neither Jew nor Greek, there can be neither slave nor freeman, there can be neither male nor female—for you are all one in Christ Jesus. (Galatians 3:25-28)

> For as with the human body which is a unity although it has many parts—all the parts of the body, though many, still making up one single body—so it is with Christ. We were baptized into one body in a single Spirit, Jews as well as Greeks, slaves as well as free men, and we were all given the same Spirit to drink....Now Christ's body is yourselves, each of you with a part to play in the whole.
> (1 Corinthians 12:12-14, 27)

> Take every care to preserve the unity of the Spirit by the peace that binds you together. There is one Body, one Spirit, just as one hope is the goal of your calling by God. There is one Lord, one faith, one baptism, and one God and Father of all, over all, through all and within all.
> (Ephesians 4:3-6)

In Pauline theology, all the baptized are clothed in the one Christ. As such, they become members of the one body of Christ, the Church. The boundaries of prejudice are shattered.

Accordingly, wives and husbands are both Church; both are living signs of Christ. In this light the exhortation divided according to sexual lines in the first century can today be applied to wife and husband on an equal basis. The Christian imperative for marriage can now validly be interpreted in this way:

1) Wives and husbands must love each other as the crucified and risen Christ loves the Church.

2) Wives and husbands must love each other as they love their own bodies, nurturing and caring for each other just as Christ tends the Church.

3) Wives and husbands must regard each other as they regard the Lord. As the Church responds to Christ, so should they respond to each other as fully as possible.

The endeavor to distinguish divine revelation from cultural assumption is further advanced when the exhortation to husband and wife is kept in the context of the whole household code. The last section deals with the relationship between slaves and masters.

> Slaves, be obedient to those who are, according to human reckoning, your masters, with deep respect and sincere loyalty, as you are obedient to Christ: not only when you are under their eye, as if you had only to please human beings, but as slaves of Christ who wholeheartedly do the will of God. Work willingly for the sake of the Lord and not for the sake of human beings. Never forget that everyone, whether a slave or a free man, will be rewarded by the Lord for whatever work he has done well. And those of you who are employers, treat your slaves in the same spirit; do without threats, and never forget that they and you have the same Master in heaven and there is no favoritism with him. (Ephesians 6:5-9)

The author here makes no attempt to challenge the institution of slavery that was so deeply imbedded in the Roman Empire of his time. Slavery was a fact of life impossible to change in the first century. What he does do is exhort Christians to bring the light of their faith to this human condition. Christian slaves are to show obedience, respect and loyalty to those over them because of their relationship with Christ, and not for the sake of people. Employers, on the other hand, are to treat their slaves in the same spirit of commitment to Christ. Slaves as well as those who are "called their masters in this world" have the same Master in heaven—who is not more impressed by one class than the other.

God's will as revealed in this text is not the condition of slavery, but rather the need to live out one's life, whether slave or free, in the spirit of Christ. Granted that slavery exists in a sin-torn world, one should respond to it in a Christian way.

The author does not promote a rebellion against slavery. He does preach a radical transformation of the slave-to-master relationship. Feelings of superiority or inferiority are to give way to a belief in equality. Threats and fears are to be replaced by a spirit of deep respect and sincere loyalty in the name of Christ. In calling for such a change in the relationship between slaves and masters, the author plants the seeds for the ultimate step, the overturn of slavery itself.

The author's handling of the slavery issue provides a key for understanding his position toward marriage in the first part of his household code. He addresses himself to the present reality without challenging cultural assumptions. He does, however, preach a radical transformation of the way Christian wives and husbands relate to each other. The cultural situation of marriage is a given. The revelation is that marriage should be experienced in the Lord. If the transformation is pursued to its logical conclusion, all division, inequality and lording it over another must give way to intimate union in the Lord.

In American society today neither biblical scholar nor ordinary believer interprets the Ephesians passage on slavery as expressing God's will that slavery be a perennial part of the human scene. By what strange quirk, then, can the parallel passage on marriage be interpreted as divine will that a husband be head of his wife, who in turn must be submissive to him?

Christian Marriage: A Sacrament

The statement, "Christian marriage is a sacrament," can sound abstract, sterile and unrelated to real life. It is helpful to break the concept down and probe its meaning in relation to the day-to-day realities of married life.

There is a twofold aspect to the reality of a sacrament. First, it is a visible, externalized, tangible experience: water flowing, bread and wine shared, forgiveness spoken. Second, the visible experience points to a reality that is invisible to mortal eyes and perceived only in faith. In Christian sacraments this unseen reality is the crucified and risen Christ present and acting upon us through the signs we make.

In Baptism, the immersion in water is death and rebirth into the Christian community, the life of Christ. The bread and wine of Eucharist is Christ present, giving us the gift of himself in intimate communion. The proclamation of forgiveness is Christ's reconciling love extended to the penitent sinner.

Marriage is a visible, tangible reality, intimately linked with the human experience. Independent of any Christian faith, it has its own rich meaning: love, the personal transformation that takes place in intimate relationship, giving and nurturing life.

In the context of Christian faith, marriage takes on further meaning: It becomes linked with the faith experience of Christ's profound love for his people. The life-enriching experience of mutual giving and receiving of two body-persons in marital love becomes a sign of the unseen, but believed, reality of Christ's gift of himself to us in intimate self-communion.

Christian marriage does not reveal this love of Christ merely in the sense of pointing it out and reminding us of it. The sacrament of marriage makes Christ's love present. Through the mutual exchange of love between wife and husband, Christ manifests his presence to the couple and enriches them with the gift of love.

There is nothing magic, however, about a sacrament. Nor is there anything magic about marriage. The experience of marriage as a Christian sacrament presupposes some degree of loving relationship with one's spouse and with Jesus Christ. Otherwise, how can a couple's relationship with each other speak to them of Christ's love relationship?

A marriage filled with hatred, disrespect and destructive personal abuse cannot be experienced as a sign of Christ's life-giving love. Some degree of those qualities associated with love must be realized in a marriage if it is to have any bearing on our perception of Christ's love for others. Only to the extent that two people grow in authentic love for each other can they be sacrament of the love that exists between Christ and his people.

An experience of marriage as a sacrament of Christ's love also presumes some level of relationship with Jesus Christ. Faith in Christ and in his love are necessary for explicit awareness of Christ's self-communication in married life. The more a person is committed in a love relationship to Jesus Christ, the more that person's commitment can be a sign of the depth and fidelity of Christ's own love.

Marriage as a sacrament of Christ's love is most clearly illustrated in the life of a couple who love each other and who find personal significance in Jesus Christ. Christ is not a distant figure far removed from their daily lives. In faith they experience his guiding presence, his compassionate understanding, his comforting love. Their relationship with Christ challenges them to express their love for each other in a Christlike manner. Their prayerful awareness of Christ's presence enables them to feel his warmth in their own love for one another.

Like all married people this ideal couple have faults and sometimes experience hurts and misunderstandings in their marital relationship. Their belief in Christ's boundless mercy leads them to work through difficult moments toward greater acceptance and forgiveness of each other. Like most persons, this couple must struggle economically, unsure of what the future holds. Neither do they escape the trials and suffering that are an integral part of family life. But through it all they find a certain peace and joy rooted in their trust in Christ's abiding presence and in their hope that in Christ all life has ultimate meaning.

Christ's Love

Talk about Christian marriage as a sign of Christ's love can remain vague and abstract if we do not describe concretely the meaning of Christ's love. What, after all, is love? Of the many characteristics that could be mentioned, the following, culled from the gospel picture of Jesus, serve a particularly important role in creating a happy marriage:

1) *Self-revelation.* Jesus invites people into relationship by revealing himself to them. He tells his disciples of his love and hopes for them. He discloses who God is for him and shares with them the values important in his life: generosity, forgiveness and prayer. He lets them know he disagrees with certain religious attitudes and legal interpretations of the religious leaders. He expresses both approval and disapproval of his disciples' behavior.

Marriage, too, is built on self-revelation—mutual self-revelation. The couple whose love is sacramental freely disclose to each other what they believe in and what they stand for. They open up to each other their fears and hopes, their dissatisfactions and desires. They share something of the meaning that God and his Kingdom have for them.

2) *Human warmth.* Jesus expresses his love in a bodily way. He hugs children and is in physical touch with women. Reaching out in body-to-body contact, he heals and consoles. He manifests his feelings in an open way. He weeps over the death of a loved one and is moved to compassion for the hungry and afflicted. He rejoices with his friends and celebrates their love with food and drink.

Marital love is also enfleshed and human. Our culture and our heritage, however, militate against freely speaking tender emotions and showing physical affection. Men hesitate to cry. Married people seem reluctant to sit close together in a car or to hold hands in public. Prolonged embraces and kisses are often confined merely to those times when married couples engage in sexual intercourse.

Christian spouses must work to overcome these cultural influences. A couple grows closer through healing touch and comforting embrace. In sorrow and in joy, in distress and in tranquility, they communicate the power of personal presence through bodily expression and bodily closeness. Such demonstrations do not happen automatically or by chance; they take determination, time and energy.

3) *Availability and service.* Jesus' purpose in life is to be for

35

others: to serve, not to be served. He washes feet and hosts a meal of bread and fish for a hungry multitude. He changes his schedule to visit the sick and to teach the gathered crowd. He spends long hours listening to others and being present to them.

Service is also a key element of marital love. A loving couple make themselves available to each other. They are willing to put their calendar aside in response to the moment's need. Listening to the other takes precedence over reading the paper. They do not feel obliged to divide chores according to stereotyped roles, but with thoughtful consideration of the pressures each feels.

4) *Fidelity*. One of the most basic and striking elements of the new covenant of Jesus' love for his people is his fidelity. When his disciples are unfairly criticized, he defends them. When they are in danger at the time of his arrest, he insists that they be allowed to go free. When death becomes the clear consequence of his preaching and healing, he embraces it in faithful dedication to God and others.

The hallmark of sacramental marriage is fidelity. In a world marked by disposable relationships and fair-weather friends, one's spouse stands as the single, last bulwark upon which one can rely. In sickness and sorrow, in joy and triumph, a faithful spouse is at one's side as comfort and companion. In the midst of unfair criticism one's spouse is one's defense. In the trials and struggles of daily living a faithful spouse gives inspiration and hope.

Such faithfulness does not come easily. It involves taking up one's cross and undergoing different kinds of dying. But only fidelity brings permanent life to the marriage and constantly gives birth to new hope for the future of the relationship.

5) *Forgiveness*. Forgiveness does not pretend that wrongs have not taken place. It does not sweep hurts under the rug. It makes no pretense that further conversion and healing are not required. Such is the forgiveness of Jesus. He confronts the Samaritan woman with her five marriages, Peter with his triple denial, the soldier with the unwarranted slap dealt him. While he forgives all sinners with understanding and compassion, he bids them go and sin no more.

Spouses need to confront each other with what is wrong, hurtful and damaging in their relationship. They should do so not in a spirit of hatred and vindictiveness, but with the hope and purpose of building a better relationship. This requires forgiveness. It also demands honest acknowledgment of guilt and a sincere desire to correct faults and to work harder at becoming more lovable.

6) *Respect for freedom.* Jesus' self-communication to others is never coercive. It always respects the person's freedom to respond in whatever way he or she chooses. Jesus leaves the rich young man free to go away and cling to his wealth. He allows Mary to respond to him in a different way than Martha. He defends a woman's right to anoint his feet with expensive perfume.

In marital love a couple freely give and receive each other as gratuitous gift. A loving couple are not manipulative or domineering. They allow for spontaneous response and creative reciprocation. They do not measure their marital responsibility in terms of mere contractual rights and legalistic obligations. The gift of marital love by one spouse calls forth the free acceptance and the free giving in return of the uniqueness of the other's being.

7) *Acknowledgment of personal dignity and equality.* One of the most remarkable aspects of Jesus' love recorded in the Gospels is his ability to transcend the social barriers of his society. He touches the leper, speaks to a Samaritan and eats with sinners. He converses with women—even those whose reputations are soiled.

A couple whose love is authentic and mature lack prejudice. They respect the dignity and equality of each other. They acknowledge the worth and God-given rights rooted in one another's personhood, irrespective of any other differences. They know but one standard that applies equally to each of them.

This section on love can best be summed up in the words of Paul to the Christians of Corinth:

> Love is always patient and kind; love is never jealous; love is not boastful or conceited, it is never rude and never seeks its own advantage, it does not take offence or store

up grievances. Love does not rejoice at wrongdoing, but finds its joy in the truth. It is always ready to make allowances, to trust, to hope and to endure whatever comes. (1 Corinthians 13:4-7)

Conclusion

We began this chapter with a look at Ephesians 5:21-33. Its author quotes the insight of Genesis 2 on becoming one flesh, describing this union as a "mystery." In Pauline theology, *mystery* or *secret* (from the Greek *mysterion*) refers to the plan of salvation for the whole human race that God has held from all eternity. Hidden in God from the beginning, this plan is revealed and put into effect in Christ Jesus. By linking this word *mysterion* with the Genesis text, which expresses the sacred nature of marriage, the Pauline author concludes that the ancient text had a hidden meaning only now understood: The bond of wife and husband, established by God long ago, foreshadowed the union of Christ and the Church.

For Christians, marriage reveals—sacramentalizes—the intimate bond of love that unites Christ and his Church. This sacramentalizing of Christ's love only *begins* in the religious ceremony of the wedding day. It is an ongoing, dynamic process realized in the couple's day-to-day, year-to-year living together. Wife and husband minister this sacrament to each other with grace-filled, transforming effects as they increasingly give of themselves to each other in saving, Christ-centered love.

For Reflection or Discussion

1) If an apostle wanted to convey to the Christians of your hometown today the same message written to the Ephesians in the first century, what would be said? What cultural assumptions might be apparent in the letter? What relationships would be addressed? What models of behavior would be offered?

2) Cite examples from recent personal experience of Christian authority—that is, the authority of loving service—in your family, your parish, your place of employment. Cite examples of "pagan" authority where one person lorded it over another. What alternative behavior would have been possible?

3) Describe Jesus Christ for someone who has never heard of him. What concept of Jesus did you stress? What does your description say about his place in your life? How does your description compare to the one your partner would offer? What impact has the relationship with Christ had on the principal relationship in your life?

4) If your relationships were the only sign (sacrament) of God's activity in the world, what would others deduce about God? What changes would you have to make for your actions to reveal the same Jesus you described above?

Partner-to-Partner Inventory

1) What is our faith understanding of Jesus Christ? How much are we able to share our faith and love of Christ with one another through discussion, shared prayer, worshiping

together? In what ways do we experience the presence and love of Christ in our relationship? In what ways do we allow Christ to inspire and influence how we treat one another?

2) What dimensions of ourselves do we reveal most easily and fully to each other? What parts of ourselves do we keep hidden from each other? How well do we think our partner reveals herself/himself? What aspects of each other would we like to get to know better?

3) How satisfied are we with the warmth and affection that we experience in our relationship? How would we like to see this area of our relationship improve?

4) How much do each of us put ourselves out for one another? How fairly do we share the various tasks and jobs around the home? Do we each assume our share of the responsibilities cheerfully and generously, or does one of us have to be pushed or nagged into doing his or her part?

5) Are we able to depend on one another to be there when one of us needs support, help and affirmation?

6) Are we able to say, "I am sorry," "I forgive you," when one of us has offended the other? Or do we sometimes bear grudges against one another?

7) Do we experience freedom to be ourselves in this relationship? Or do we feel unnecessary constraints? Do we leave each other free to grow in our uniqueness? What unnecessary constraints do we put on one another?

PRAYER SERVICE

Sign of Christ's Love

For this service have a lighted candle, preferably one in a multi-colored glass container.

Opening Prayer

Lord Jesus, you are the light of the world. You let your light shine through your warm compassionate love for humankind. In this way you reveal to us the love of God, the God who is Love. Help us to manifest your love through the love we express toward one another. We ask this, Lord, in your name. Amen.

Scripture Reading

> My dear friends,
> this is not a new commandment I am writing for you,
> but an old commandment
> that you have had from the beginning;
> the old commandment is the message you have heard.
> Yet in another way, I am writing a new commandment for
>   you
> —and this is true for you, just as much as for him—
> for darkness is passing away
> and the true light is already shining.
> Whoever claims to be in light
> but hates his brother
> is still in darkness.
> Anyone who loves his brother remains in light
> and there is in him nothing to make him fall away.
> (1 John 2:7-10)

Silent reflection

Sharing of thoughts on the reading

Litany

This Litany reflects three different moods: thanksgiving, penitence and resolution. Couples should pause between the sections and allow themselves to settle into the mood of the prayer.

For calling us to be partners in this Christian marriage,
　　We thank you, Lord.

For allowing us to know your presence
in our presence to one another,
　　We thank you, Lord.

For inspiring us to reflect your love in our marital love,
　　We thank you, Lord.

For the sacrament we have been for each other,
　　We thank you, Lord.

For the times when we have failed to show Christ-like love
in our marriage,
　　Lord, have mercy.

For the ways in which we have lacked human warmth
and sensitivity,
　　Lord, have mercy.

For the occasions when we have been reluctant
to serve each other's needs,
　　Lord, have mercy.

For our lack of forgiveness and compassion,
　　Lord, have mercy.

We will strive to grow in our faith and love of Christ,
　　Lord, help us, we pray.

We wish to give fuller sign of Christ's love in our relationship,
Lord, help us, we pray.

The couple add further resolutions of their own.
Lord, help us, we pray.

Light Ceremony

Each partner, in turn, takes the lighted candle and hands it to the other, saying these or similar words:

N._____, I give you this candle as sign of the light I will continue to strive to be for you.

Response: I am grateful for the light you are to me.

Concluding Prayer

(Refrain is recited together. The verses, taken from John 15:9-14 (NAB), can be recited by either spouse.)

Refrain: Arise, shine out, for your light has come,
and the glory of Yahweh has risen on you. (Isaiah 60:1)

As the Father loves me, so I also love you.
Remain in my love.

Refrain

If you keep my commandments, you will remain in my love,
just as I have kept my Father's commandments
and remain in his love.

Refrain

I have told you this so that my joy might be in you and your joy might be complete.

Refrain

This is my commandment: love one another
as I love you.

Refrain

No one has greater love than this,
to lay down one's life for one's friends.
You are my friends
if you do what I command you.

Refrain

Glory be to the Father,
and to the Son,
and to the Holy Spirit,
as it was in the beginning,
is now,
and ever shall be,
world without end. Amen.

Kiss of Peace

THE KINGDOM OF HEAVEN may be compared to a king who gave a feast for his son's wedding. (Matthew 22:2)

The kingdom of Heaven is like treasure hidden in a field which someone has found; he hides it again, goes off in his joy, sells everything he owns and buys the field.
(Matthew 13:44)

Again, the kingdom of Heaven is like a merchant looking for fine pearls; when he finds one of great value he goes and sells everything he owns and buys it.
(Matthew 13:45-46)

THREE

Marriage and the Kingdom of God

Wₑ live in a world marked by contradictory forces. The human environment is plagued with wars, oppression and exploitation, by murder, rape and theft. Yet human beings daily push back the horizons of beauty, self-sacrifice and learning, striving for love and intimate communion.

As a human family we find ourselves pulled in opposite directions, wondering what it all means and where it will all end. Will humankind, empowered with nuclear weapons, wipe itself off the face of the earth in an ultimate act of madness? Or will the noble and the good within us somehow rise up and take command of the world situation and lead us into a new age where we will hammer our swords into plowshares and peacefully sit under the vine and fig tree (see Micah 4:3-4)?

From a Christian perspective, the answer to the question depends on how open humans are to the Kingdom of God proclaimed by Jesus Christ. In the words of the Preface for the Feast of Christ the King, echoed by the Second Vatican Council, it is:

a kingdom of truth and life,
a kingdom of holiness and grace,
a kingdom of justice, love and peace.

What is the significance of this Kingdom for human life? How does experiencing the Kingdom in marriage relate to establishing God's reign in human society today? How are the qualities linked with God's Kingdom significant for richer, happier marriages?

God's Reign and Human Life

God reigns among human beings to the degree that we allow God to influence our minds, hearts and actions. We come under God's influence when we freely respond to God's gratuitous love and gift of self in friendship. As we respond, God transforms us. God turns our hearts from self-centeredness to generosity and sensitivity, from prejudice to understanding, from apathy to love and concern.

The change God works within us was described by the prophet Ezekiel:

I shall give you a new heart, and put a new spirit in you;
I shall remove the heart of stone from your bodies and
give you a heart of flesh instead. (Ezekiel 36:26)

The reign of God is fully and visibly manifested in Jesus Christ. In Christ the Word of God has become flesh; in him God's dream of intimate relationship with humanity has become reality. Jesus knows God in extraordinary intimacy within the depths of his being. He calls God *Abba*, "Father." Jesus' love for God enables him to embrace all people as sisters and brothers. It does not matter whether they are friends or enemies, virtuous or sinful, socially acceptable or outcast. Christ prays for them all, forgives them, and invites them to form a new community of love.

Christ, through his ministry, his death and resurrection and his gift of the Spirit, makes it possible for us to come to God as daughters and sons and to draw close to one another as sisters and brothers. In Christ the Kingdom of God is already in our midst. Yet the reign of God is incomplete until we fully accept the Spirit of Christ, the Spirit of truth and love. By striving to give evidence in our lives of the justice and peace, honesty and love Christ enfleshes, we further the reign of God in the world today, and thus prepare for the ultimate fulfillment of God's Kingdom.

The central mission of the Christian community is to give conscious and explicit witness to the Kingdom proclaimed by Jesus. Its members are called to announce the Good News that God is already at work in all humanity, gradually drawing the entire human family into the kind of personal communion with God and with each other that the Father and Jesus enjoy.

God's Reign in Marriage

Christian marriage is intrinsically part of this mission to further God's reign. A couple is called to live out their personal commitment to Christ by dedicating themselves to each other and forming a human community, a family. In this way they experience God's presence and influence at work in their lives. By growing in honesty and loving self-sacrifice in their own relationship, they advance the truthfulness, justice and unity that God desires all humanity to achieve.

What happens in a marriage is critical for the promotion of God's Kingdom on earth. If two people who choose each other out of love cannot work through life's difficulties and achieve a meaningful level of peace and unity, how can the great human conglomerate realistically be expected to achieve harmony? If couples end up destroying rather than saving each other, what does this bode for the diversity of people who share a small planet? On the other hand, the sacrificial and loving union of a married couple can give new hope for all humanity and, like leaven, contributes to genuine human community worldwide.

The reign of God is not an abstraction. It has concrete, practical implications for enriching the quality of a marital relationship. These can be explicated by applying to marriage the seven characteristics the liturgy associates with the Kingdom of Christ in the passage cited on p. 48.

1) *Truth.* Truthfulness is much more than not telling a lie. It means sharing one's perception of reality with another. It involves communicating one's thoughts and feelings, hopes and disappointments, sorrows and joys. And since no person is an isolated unit, but finds full meaning in terms of relationship with God, with parents and siblings, with neighbors, friends and enemies, these dynamics become part of the communication of self.

Fostering truth in marriage also implies listening to each other. Listening involves sympathetic understanding: "I know what you are saying. I feel what you are feeling. I appreciate where you are coming from." Listening requires respect: "I acknowledge that what you have to say is as important as what I have to say." Listening is rooted in personal interest: "I really care about what is going on within you and very much wish you to communicate this."

Truthfulness, however, should not be confused with "letting it all hang out." In order for communication of truth to serve marital growth, it must be done *in love.* Truth without love is destructive. Truthfulness in love enables a person to discern when to speak and when to remain silent. It helps one decide when the faults of another should be confronted and when they should be overlooked. It guides one in judging which skeletons in the closet (e.g., an earlier affair, a former pregnancy or abortion, a previous encounter with the law) should be brought to light, and which should be left buried.

2) *Life.* Human life is much more than mere physical existence. Our inborn capacities for freedom, knowledge, love, relationship and self-determination distinguish us from the rest of the animal kingdom. The more these powers are exercised and enjoyed, the more fully alive a person becomes.

Marriage provides the most intimate possibilities for touching and enriching the inner life of a person. In marriage we freely give ourselves to one another. We open ourselves in

50

receptivity to the gift of the other. We make a covenant whereby each of us may enter, spiritually as well as physically, into the inner dimensions of the other's being where no one else is allowed to intrude. In this unique communion between spouses, we come to know and love ourselves with greater security. We are thus enabled to enter into deeper communion with God and to reach out with renewed energy to other members of the human family.

3) *Holiness.* Holiness is allowing God to fill us with his love and affect the way we relate to everyone else. For Christians, holiness is rooted in friendship with Jesus Christ. Christ introduces God as Father and gifts us with the power of the Spirit. In Christ all people become our sisters and our brothers.

In marriage the Christian couple nourish each other's holiness by sharing their experience of God and of Jesus Christ. They need to communicate to each other the meaning of their faith—and also their questions and doubts. They need to share prayer, not only by reciting prayers together, but by giving to each other a glimpse of their inner prayer life. This means they let each other see who God is for them, the inspiration born of their religious experience. They share their journey of faith and their vision of where it leads.

Most poignantly, a couple affects each other's holiness by manifesting the intimate presence of God. They do this by their own appreciation, love and regard for one another.

4) *Grace.* Grace is gift. It is graciousness and gracefulness. It is gratuitous. Grace is favor and kindness.

Biblically, the ultimate grace is the free gift of God's self to us in kindness and in faithful bond of love. In the New Testament God gives this gift in the fullest way in the enfleshment of God's own Word, Jesus Christ.

The preceding chapter spoke of the covenant of marriage for Christians being a sign, a sacrament of the covenant of God's self-gift to us in Jesus Christ. Thus a couple makes God's grace visible every time they grace each other with love and concern, favor and kindness, giving and keeping their word to one another. They are grace to each other in their gracious response to one another's needs, their gratitude for each other's uniqueness and their courteous, graceful manners.

5) *Justice.* Too easily we make the mistake of setting justice and love in opposition to each other. Love, to be sure, goes far beyond justice, but love without justice fails to be authentic.

Practicing justice means respecting the rights of another. It is acting toward the other in an equitable, upright way. It is too easy to overlook justice in the name of "love."

Ironically, some of the greatest violations of justice take place in marriage; it is far easier to become concerned about justice in the world than at home. It is possible to be sincerely concerned about global respect for human rights yet remain blind to the human rights violations under one's own roof.

Every couple needs to examine how they promote or violate justice in their marriage. Does one spouse offend the personal dignity of the other in thought, word or action? Does one make decisions that both should make? Does each respect the other's conscience? Do sexist views intrude on the marriage? Does each give the other everything he or she is entitled to by virtue of the marriage commitment? Does each assume a fair share of the chores and burdens that go with living together?

6) *Love.* Sin is human alienation from God and from one another. Sin is the refusal to walk with God, the refusal to be life for each other. It is hatred. It is death.

The love of God takes sin away and gives humans new life (see 1 John 4:9-10). The love of God is the foundation for marital love. When wife and husband love each other they make God's love come alive in their relationship. They walk hand in hand, conquering the alienation that splits the world apart. They reject the darkness of isolation, suspicion and pettiness; they choose the light of intimacy, trust and generosity. Their supportive life deals a death blow to exploitation and competition by inviting each to dare take the risk of becoming all he or she is called to be.

7) *Peace.* Peace is not a state to be preserved at any price, but a dynamic quality that must constantly be created anew. Peace is not a passive tranquility that should never be disturbed. Rather,

it grows gradually at the price of honest encounter and constructive confrontation.

It is significant that Christ, who came to bring peace, also became a sign of division. Proclaiming the Kingdom of God, Jesus stated that the happy ones who shall be called the children of God are the peace*makers* (see Matthew 5:9). He did not say peace*keepers*.

Married couples are called to a life of peace (see 1 Corinthians 7:15). This peace is never achieved by burying hurts and grievances and allowing wounded feelings to build up inside. A couple must take the risk of expressing justified anger and pointing to what is wrong. A good, fair fight has a place in the painful process of creating peace. If these measures are taken in a spirit of mutual honesty, charity and forgiveness, they will foster marital union rather than strain it.

The Reign of God and Happiness in Marriage

The qualities associated with God's Kingdom make the difference between happiness or misery in marriage. The realities that especially cause unhappiness in a marriage and those that contribute to a satisfying marital relationship can be measured against the Kingdom traits of truthfulness, life and love, grace and holiness, justice and peace.

The following parallel columns contrast the absence of these characteristics with their presence. The different marital "portraits" that result are deliberately depicted in stark contrast, in order to make the point. Obviously, no marriage will fall completely under one column or the other. All marriages will fall somewhere between the two.

Deficiencies in Truthfulness

Our marriage is marked by secretiveness, deception, two-facedness.

Experiences of Truthfulness

We express our opinions about each other, about the marriage, family problems, our work.

We experience long periods of moody silence.

We are unable to talk to each other about anything significant. If we express our opinions or feelings, we meet with ridicule.

We do not share our deeper thoughts and feelings.

We are unable to bring each other to understand and accept the truth of who we are and what we stand for.

When we need to confront each other and air our grievances, we are fair, and aim our confrontation at the building of a better relationship.

We discuss our diverse views on politics, religion, world affairs, respecting each other's right to hold a different perspective.

We express our joy and our sorrow, our silly moods and our serious ones, and know we'll be accepted. We share the things that are important to us as persons.

We enjoy our silent moments together. In our silence we intuit the beauty, the goodness and the love that exists between us. In our silence we know we understand.

Deficiencies in Life and Love

We coexist, strangers in our own house, at a distance from one another, each going our separate ways. Never is there a meeting of our deeper selves.

We exist in coldness. We chill each other to the core of our being.

Our hostile feelings have become so pent up that we have built a wall between us.

We exist under the same roof in hatred, enemies at war.

When we are together, we can't wait until we are apart.

Experiences of Life and Love

We are independent, mature beings whose lives are intertwined. The presence of one another lights up our lives.

In each other we find security, trust and much future promise.

We are sensitive to each other's feelings and needs.

We support the good in each other.

We enjoy each other's company. We are deeply "in love."

Deficiencies in Grace and Holiness

Our marriage is an obligation that we are stuck with. It is duty and drudgery.

Our marriage is stifling. It is destructive of our personalities.

We grumble and show discontent when asked to do something for each other.

God's love and God's gift of self has little or no influence on the way we experience our lives together.

Experiences of Grace and Holiness

Our marriage is a most important gift in our lives. We are God's gift, God's grace to each other.

Our marriage is for both of us an opportunity for growth and enrichment.

We look upon our responsibilities as opportunities to be and do for each other.

We are gracious and graceful in our dealings with each other.

Deficiencies in Justice and Peace

We quarrel most of the time.

We experience ridicule and belittling of our self-image.

We do not help each other or cooperate with the chores.

There is constant repression regarding what one can do, where one can go, to whom one can speak.

We fight unfairly, deliberately hurting the other's feelings.

There is physical violence: throwing things, use of force, blows. We exploit each other sexually.

Experiences of Justice and Peace

We can discuss our disagreements calmly and with understanding.

We promote in each other a healthy self-image and a good feeling about ourselves.

We go out of our way to be generous to each other.

We respect each other's privacy. We give each other space. We have regard for each other's conscience.

We are sensitive to each other's feelings and needs.

We show respect for each other's body.

The contrasts underscore the fact that the Kingdom Christ proclaims is not a merely future event for which we passively wait. The reign of God affects the quality of married life here and now. We create happiness in our marriage by building our relationship on the very virtues that Christ calls for when he insists,

> The kingdom of God is at hand. Repent, and believe in the gospel. (Mark 1:15, NAB)

A Happy Marriage, a Better World

Marriage—the foundation of the family—is the basic unit of human community. Most of the human race chooses to remain in a family setting. The quality of life and relationship that is found within marriages and families, then, intimately affects the well-being of the whole human environment. By allowing God to reign in their lives and by displaying Kingdom values in their relationship, married people better their neighborhood, their Church and the wider global community.

This is true because married people are so numerous in the neighborhood, the Church and the world. It is also true because a loving marriage enables a couple to share themselves more effectively with the wider community.

For instance, one of the requirements for bettering any group—Church, school, corporation or neighborhood—is the ability to speak one's mind, to confront injustices and unthinking policies, to stand up and be counted in controversy. A couple who learn to communicate intimately and who are unafraid of necessary confrontation gain the experience and courage to use these same communication skills in other groups.

Another example is in the area of compassionate love. Every community has its suffering people who hunger for understanding, sympathy and concern. Apathy is their great enemy. In marital love a couple comes into unique touch with each other's frustrations, the hurts and yearnings within the human heart. They grow in empathy, gaining a sense of what it means to be in the other's situation. Such experiences can enable them to bring deeper empathy to needs in the broader community.

One of the crises facing parish communities is dissatisfaction with the liturgy. Many worshipers feel distant from one another; their group prayer reflects very little true faith-sharing. Learning to share the deeply personal dimension of religious life with a spouse prepares a couple for greater openness with the worshiping community. Not content with hiding behind mere recitation of congregational prayers, such couples can help create worship services that speak to the personal beliefs, doubts and faith commitments of other adults.

A final illustration of a happily married couple's contribution to the wider community concerns sexual equality. Discrimination against women is an unfortunate reality that continues to mar major areas of contemporary society. Many men are afraid of women; they are threatened by loss of control. In turn, some women submit to male dominance, while others become hostile to men in general.

In marriages where stereotypes and prejudices are put aside, the couple accept each other as persons who are equal in human dignity. They learn not to be threatened by the opposite sex. They come to appreciate more the complementarity of diverse sexual perspectives and approaches to life. They become copartners on a lifelong journey.

Such an experience of equality in marriage helps purge spouses of sexist tendencies. A man who is comfortably living on an equal plane with his wife is better able to relate to women with fairness and respect at work or in political and social circles. A woman who is treated as an equal by the husband she loves will be better able to assert herself in other circumstances without pettiness or hostility. Achievement of sexual equality in marriage will advance sexual equality in all facets of human life.

Conclusion

Truth and life, holiness and grace, justice, love and peace are the realities that spell the difference between heaven and hell in this life as well as in the next. The choice is ours. When married couples enflesh Kingdom qualities in their relationship they taste something of God's life now. They also contribute to the humanization of the earth and advance the human race toward "the kingdom prepared for you since the foundation of the world" (Matthew 25:34).

For Reflection or Discussion

1) Reflect how the qualities associated with the Kingdom of God have enriched your relationships. Which qualities seem most deficient? What practical steps might you take to realize these characteristics more fully?

2) If you had infinite power, what changes would you make in the world, the Church, your family to bring those communities into closer harmony with the Kingdom of God? What contribution toward those ends lies within your power right now?

3) Compare the efforts you would like to see the world make to achieve justice and peace for all persons with the effort you make within the confines of your own home.

4) Recall a recent situation in which you gained from meeting truth blended with love. Recall a situation in which you used truth without love and consider how you might respond differently in a similar situation.

Partner-to-Partner Inventory

1) What practical meaning does the Kingdom (reign) of God have for our daily lives?

2) Do we understand our relationship as a significant way in which we can experience and promote the Kingdom of God?

3) How are the various qualities of God's kingdom reflected or not reflected in our relationship in light of the columns on pages 53-55?

The Reign of God

Opening Prayer

Lord Jesus, the heart of your ministry was proclaiming the reign of God among us. One of the symbols you chose to describe God's kingdom was the wedding feast. Help us to allow God's love and goodness to reign in our marriage, and in our relationships with those whose lives we touch. We pray this, Lord, in your name. Amen.

Scripture Reading

As the chosen of God, then, the holy people whom he loves, you are to be clothed in heartfelt compassion, in generosity and humility, gentleness and patience. Bear with one another; forgive each other if one of you has a complaint against another. The Lord has forgiven you; now you must do the same. Over all these clothes, put on love, the perfect bond. And may the peace of Christ reign in your hearts, because it is for this that you were called together in one body. Always be thankful.

Let the Word of Christ, in all its richness, find a home with you. Teach each other, and advise each other, in all wisdom. With gratitude in your hearts sing psalms and hymns and inspired songs to God; and whatever you say or do, let it be in the name of the Lord Jesus, in thanksgiving to God the Father through him.

(Colossians 3:12-17)

Silent reflection

Sharing of thoughts on the reading

Litany

This Litany reflects three different moods: thanksgiving, penitence and resolution. Couples should pause between the sections and allow themselves to settle into the mood of the prayer.

For all the ways we have experienced your grace
in our marriage,
    We thank you, Lord.

For the love we have achieved,
    We thank you, Lord.

For the gift of honesty with one another,
    We thank you, Lord.

For the strength you have given us
to create peace in our lives,
    We thank you, Lord.

For the times we were not open to the influence
of your love,
    Lord, have mercy.

For the occasions when we have not communicated honestly
with one another,
    Lord, have mercy.

For the times when our words and actions caused hurt,
rather than healing,
and disturbance, rather than peace,
    Lord, have mercy.

For any unfairness toward each other,
    Lord, have mercy.

We recommit ourselves to be open to your grace
in our lives,
    Lord, help us, we pray.

We will work more diligently in making our home
a place of peace and love,
> Lord, help us, we pray.

The couple add further resolutions of their own.
> Lord, help us, we pray.

Concluding Prayer

(Recite together.)

Father, all-powerful and ever-living God,
we do well always and everywhere to give you thanks.

You anointed Jesus Christ, your only Son, with the oil of gladness,
as the eternal priest and universal king....

As king he claims dominion over all creation,
that he may present to you, his almighty Father,
an eternal and universal kingdom:
a kingdom of truth and life,
a kingdom of holiness and grace,
a kingdom of justice, love, and peace.

And so, with all the choirs of angels in heaven
we proclaim your glory
and join in their unending hymn of praise:

Holy, holy, holy Lord, God of power and might,
heaven and earth are full of your glory.
> Hosanna in the highest.
Blessed is he who comes in the name of the Lord.
> Hosanna in the highest.
> (From the Preface for the Feast of Christ the King.)

Kiss of Peace

BEFORE THE FESTIVAL of the Passover, Jesus, knowing that his hour had come to pass from this world to the Father, having loved those who were his in the world, loved them to the end.

They were at supper, and the devil had already put it into the mind of Judas Iscariot, son of Simon, to betray him. Jesus knew that the Father had put everything into his hands, and that he had come from God and was returning to God, and he got up from table, removed his outer garments and, taking a towel, wrapped it round his waist; he then poured water into a basin and began to wash the disciples' feet and to wipe them with the towel he was wearing.

He came to Simon Peter, who said to him, "Lord, are you going to wash my feet?" Jesus answered, "At the moment you do not know what I am doing, but later you will understand," "Never!" said Peter, "You shall never wash my feet." Jesus replied, "If I do not wash you, you can have no share with me." Simon Peter said, "Well then, Lord, not only my feet, but my hands and my head as well!" Jesus said, "No one who has had a bath needs washing, such a person is clean all over...."

When he had washed their feet and put on his outer garments again he went back to the table. "Do you understand," he said, "what I have done to you? You call me Master and Lord, and rightly; so I am. If I, then, the Lord and Master, have washed your feet, you must wash each other's feet. I have given you an example so that you may copy what I have done to you."

(John 13:1-10a, 12-15)

FOUR

Marriage as Ministry

It would be interesting to stand
outside a church on Sunday and ask people at random what
images immediately flash before their minds when they hear the
word *ministry*. The most prominent answers would undoubtedly
include the priest at the altar, the deacon in the pulpit, the
minister by a deathbed. A few with a broader concept of ministry
might also mention the nun running an orphanage, the brother
working with the poor in Appalachia or the lay volunteer teaching
Mexican-Americans in San Antonio.

How many persons would include among their images of
ministry a wife and husband making love, a mother picking
daisies with her five-year-old, a father changing his infant's
diapers? Including these last three examples as an important part
of ministry might be a little startling. But if we take the
sacramentality of marriage seriously, then whatever goes into the
building of a happy family must be viewed as an authentic form
of ministry.

Three basic presuppositions underlie our discussion of
marriage as ministry. First, proclaiming the reign of God was the
central focus of Jesus' teaching and healing ministry. Furthering

65

the Kingdom continues to be the heart of the ongoing ministry of the risen Christ.

Second, as the Vatican Council points out in the *Constitution on the Church, all* baptized women and men share in the priesthood and prophetic office of Jesus Christ. Christians exercise this ministry in diverse ways according to the variety of gifts each has received:

> The baptized, by regeneration and the anointing of the Holy Spirit, are consecrated into a spiritual house and a holy priesthood....
>
> Though they differ from one another in essence and not only in degree, the common priesthood of the faithful and the ministerial or hierarchical priesthood are nonetheless interrelated. Each of them in its own special way is a participation in the one priesthood of Christ. The ministerial priest, by the sacred power he enjoys, molds and rules the priestly people. Acting in the person of Christ, he brings about the Eucharistic Sacrifice, and offers it to God in the name of all the people. For their part, the faithful join in the offering of the Eucharist by virtue of their royal priesthood. They likewise exercise that priesthood by receiving the sacraments, by prayer and thanksgiving, by the witness of a holy life, and by self-denial and active charity. (#10)
>
> The holy People of God shares also in Christ's prophetic office. It spreads abroad a living witness to Him, especially by means of a life of faith and charity and by offering to God a sacrifice of praise, the tribute of lips which give honor to His name. (#12)

Third, married people share in the ministry of Christ in their own way. As Vatican II points out, spouses help each other grow in holiness in their married life. In their way of life, by their word and example, parents are supposed to be "the first preachers of the faith to their children." "The family is, so to speak, the domestic Church" (*Constitution on the Church*, #11).

Ministry to Each Other

Administering the sacraments constitutes a significant element of Christian ministry in the Catholic tradition. In the sacrament of marriage the ministers are the spouses themselves; the priest is merely the official witness. This means that spouses begin their married life as sacramental ministers to one another.

As we saw in Chapter Two, the sacrament of marriage is not completed once the spouses say "I do" at the ceremony. Their entire marriage is a sacrament that they minister to each other.

In specific terms, what does this sacramental ministry involve? An answer begins to emerge when we reflect on what we mean by Christian ministry in general. Seven components come to mind: strengthening faith commitment, teaching, counseling, affirming a person's self-image, lightening another's burdens, healing and comforting.

Certainly these elements are found in the ministry of Jesus. He invites people to a new faith relationship with God. He teaches the crowds in the Temple and on the hillside what it means to follow him. His disciples receive guidance and advice regarding the course of action they should pursue. Outcasts discover that Jesus ignores the social discriminations that isolate them; he sees them as worthwhile human beings. Jesus helps the suffering through their struggles. He heals the sinful and the sick. In him those mourning the death of a loved one find comfort.

When we examine the work of the priest or ordained minister we recognize similar components. Ordained ministry is not merely a matter of presiding at worship services and preaching from the pulpit. The average priest or minister spends many hours in individual counseling sessions, as well as beside hospital beds and in funeral parlors.

In the context of this general understanding of Christian ministry, we can reflect on the life of a married couple as sacramental ministry. The same seven aspects of ministry already mentioned can serve as the framework for presenting some examples of how a wife and husband minister to each other.

1) *Strengthening faith*. In their intimate living situation a couple constantly witness to each other the beliefs and values that give direction to their lives. They reveal to one another what inspires them to make sacrifices and what encourages them to keep on going despite struggle or routine. No one can believe for another. No one can *prove* that another's faith in God, in Christ, in risen life is founded in reality. But a spouse's faith and the enrichment it brings help make one's own leap of faith seem reasonable despite all the disbelief in the world around us.

2) *Teaching*. In a love relationship I not only reveal who I am to you but also who you are to me. In the light of what you mean to me, I further reveal you to yourself. This is the central kind of teaching spouses offer each other. In the context of their love for one another they both learn better who they are, with their strengths and weaknesses, their virtues and faults, their possibilities and limitations. Such learning from one another becomes an important base for personal growth and enrichment.

3) *Counseling*. One of the essential requirements for counseling is knowledge and understanding of the individual person. Because of their intimate knowledge of each other, spouses can give sound advice in many areas of human conduct and decision-making. Often one spouse serves as a significant balance to the other, checking a tendency to be impetuous for instance, or encouraging one inclined to be fearful and overprotective.

4) *Affirmation*. Many people fail to realize their potential because they do not believe in themselves, their worth and their power for good. When spouses stand by one another with love and faith, they help each other to feel good about themselves and to get in touch with their own inner strengths and talents. Acceptance by one's spouse provides courage and freedom to dare be oneself even at the risk of being rejected by others.

5) *Easing burdens*. One of the most appealing sayings recorded in the Gospels is Christ's open invitation, "Come to me, all you who labor and are overburdened, and I will give you rest" (Matthew 11:28). An integral part of the ministry that a couple

extend to each other consists in lightening the burdens built into daily life and work. The couple engage in this dimension of ministry first by the appreciation, understanding and sympathy they express toward one another. They communicate that they know what it is like to be home with small children all day, or to endure the routine of the office or the monotony of the factory. Both spouses further ease the burdens of daily living by generously sharing the workload of endless chores (shopping, cleaing bathrooms, washing dishes, to name a few).

6) *Healing.* Through their personal intimacy spouses heal each other from the hurts, frustrations and hardships that result from dealings with the wider world. Husband and wife also heal each other by forgiving the failings, misunderstandings and faults that occur in their own relationship. By their concern and care they help each other through illness and provide for general growth in health and well-being. Finally, spouses aid each other in the healing of painful memories that continue to haunt one from earlier times, gently drawing each other into a happier present and a hope-filled future.

7) *Comforting.* Spouses are in the most privileged position to offer renewed hope when one is disappointed because plans for achievement and success have not materialized. They can provide solace and support in times of painful conflicts with relatives or coworkers. One's spouse becomes the most important source of comfort in time of mourning over the death of a parent, a sibling, a child.

Ministry to Children

The marital relationship is not merely an important prelude to having children. Everything a couple do to build a warmer, more loving and lasting relationship already constitutes an authentic form of Christian ministry. The most effective way that a couple can minister to their children is by first having a good marriage. In their love for one another they love their children. In their children they love one another.

Their parents' love for each other teaches children what marriage, love and human sexuality are all about. Their parents' marriage is the model which, while not to be blindly imitated, serves as a guide in shaping their ideals. Perceiving the sexual love that exists between their parents, children intuit the link between human sexuality and responsible love and commitment. Experiencing the respect with which their parents treat each other, children learn the dignity of members of the opposite sex.

Their parents' fidelity and warmly expressed affection for one another create an atmosphere of permanence and security that children can depend on. In such an environment children come to believe that they, too, are loved and precious. This enables them to believe in themselves and to take the risk of growing in their own uniqueness.

Of course, married people also minister directly to their children. It must be kept in mind that this parental ministry is as much a part of fatherhood as it is of motherhood. In our male-dominated culture we have emphasized the nature of women to be mothers and to be present in the home and to care for their children. The time is long overdue to give similar emphasis to the nature of men to be fathers, and their *equal* responsibility to be present in the home and to be involved in the nurturing of their children. With this important point in mind we can probe some of the significant aspects of parental ministry to the spiritual, emotional and physical needs of the child.

1) *Acceptance*. This begins with acceptance of a pregnancy, even an unplanned one. A child deserves welcome as an individual. Girl or boy, healthy or disabled, each child is a unique composite of characteristics, talents and limitations. Parents who nourish the specialness of *this* child without trying to force the child into a preconceived mold allow the best to come forth from within the child's very own being.

This acceptance is an integral part of parenting a child through every stage of growth. In the pattern of Christ's ministry, parents accept the joys and pangs, the beauty and the rough edges, what is graceful and what is awkward in the diverse periods of development through infancy, childhood and adolescence. While they encourage the good and discourage the bad, the message of acceptance and love is unambiguously clear.

2) *Presence.* Perhaps the most costly and most rewarding dimension of parental ministry is investing time and psychic energy in being personally present to children. Physical presence is a matter of merely being in the same place as another. Personal presence involves being there *for* children, offering oneself in communicative gift to them and being responsive to their self-giving and communication.

Being present to children in this way takes many forms: playing with them, openly demonstrating affection, taking seriously what they have to say, answering their questions honestly and on the appropriate level, sharing walks, and becoming a creative and integral part of family activities. When children are small, personal presence means reading and listening to stories, wiping tears, sharing treats and encouraging the latest accomplishment in art, roller-skating and cycling. As the children grow older, personal presence manifests itself by being willing to listen to them when they come in late at night, bearing with them through their struggles, inviting free expression of opinion and sharing with them on a deep level insights born out of one's own experience.

3) *Physical care.* In John's Gospel Jesus washes his disciples' feet to symbolize the Christian call to ministry (see John 13:1-15). In Matthew our concern for human needs is presented as the basis of the final judgment and enhanced by Christ identifying himself with those in need. The ministry rewarded by heavenly inheritance includes feeding the hungry, giving drink to the thirsty, clothing the naked and visiting the sick (see Matthew 25:34-40).

Tending to the physical needs of others is no less a ministry when performed for members of one's own family. Fathers and mothers minister to their children in all the ordinary, physical tasks so essential to human growth and happiness: giving baths, preparing endless meals, keeping ahead of the laundry, staying up long nights with crying infants and sick children. The effectiveness of this ministry is extraordinarily enhanced when the parents perform these tasks with generous love, sensitive concern and graceful gentleness.

4) *Religious formation.* Parents are the primary religious educators of their children. Parents who manifest their faith-commitment to Christ in their family life create an atmosphere which inspires and nourishes their children's faith. In this context all ordinary ministering is a sign of the parents' Christian life, and hence helps nurture the Christ-life in the child. Religion is more "caught" than taught. Children simply absorb the religious environment of the home.

In a more formal way, parents nurture faith in their children by bringing them into their own family prayer at an early age. They nurture faith by being unafraid to share their own beliefs and values with their children, by addressing themselves to their children's religious questions and showing patience and understanding in the face of doubts. Even when "professionals" become involved in the work of religious education, these parents do not abrogate their responsibility, but insist on their primary role in the sacramental preparation and in the ongoing religious education of their children.

Ministry to the Wider Community

Sometimes so much emphasis is put on how members of the family can participate in the ministry of the Church outside the home that the ministerial dimension within family life itself becomes obscured. That is why the first concern of this chapter has been the ministry to our spouses and children. On the other hand, it would be a serious mistake to limit our notion of marital ministry to life within the family. The family does not exist solely for its own sake, but also for building up the whole human community. Ministry within the family should enable its members to minister in a significant way to the wider community.

One principal way the family extends itself in service is

through the work that provides its financial support. Some professions—education, caring for the sick, social services—are obviously connected with the ongoing ministry of Christ. For a Christian, however, any paid occupation, whether in the factory, in a trade or in the business world, should have a ministerial or apostolic dimension. Such work is not only the means of livelihood, but also a way for baptized persons to manifest their ideals of faith, justice, love and caring service.

Another way the family ministers to the wider community is through voluntary services. This can be informal service to relatives, friends and neighbors: providing hospitality, driving an elderly person to the shopping plaza, phoning a semi-invalid. The family also serves the community more formally by membership in organizations that minister to the poor, the disabled and the emotionally distressed.

Church-related activities provide numerous opportunities for family involvements. Married couples can add an important dimension to programs for the engaged, the newlywed, and for those having difficulty in their marriage. Parents offer a significant contribution to the design and operation of parish school and religious education programs, as well as to other youth-oriented activities. It is appropriate for families to be involved in the liturgy as readers, distributors and servers.

In choosing ways to minister to the wider community, a couple must consider a few principles. How much time and energy each is going to expend outside the home must be mutually decided on the basis of interests and talents of both spouses, and on the needs of the household. Stereotyping sex roles only limits a family's reach; justice demands that both partners create for each other opportunities for involvement, whether for pay or as a volunteer. Especially when both spouses work outside the home both must share responsibilities and chores within the family.

Both spouses need to be in touch with their priorities and their motivation. Is it more important to maintain family relationships or to climb the promotional ladder? How do they balance their primary responsibilities to each other and the children with the Christian responsibility for the needs of those outside the family? If one stays at home, is it because of dedication to the family or fear of outside involvement? If one engages in many outside activities, does the involvement flow from the commitment to spouse and children, or is it an escape from them?

Supporting Marital Ministry

Just as married people and families have a responsibility toward the wider human community, so the reverse is true. Couples need communal support and help to build a strong marriage and a sound family life. There are a number of ways in which the Church, the government and society in general can better aid married people in their ministry.

The first important support the Church can give to married people is to recognize in practice what it acknowledges in words: that married couples are called to holiness and to participation in the ministry of Christ. "Vocation Sundays" could celebrate and promote the vocation to marriage as well as the call to priesthood or religious life. Why not pray for an increase of dedicated married people, as well as for more sisters and priests?

The ongoing discussion about admitting married people to ordained ministry needs to take place in the context of a theology of marriage as a prophetic, priestly and sacramental ministry. The tendency thus far has often been to divorce such discussions from these important theological underpinnings. In arguing for the value of celibacy, more care could be taken in Catholic circles to avoid giving the impression that marriage is an obstacle to full dedication to Christ and to the work of the Church.

Even as the discussion of ordained ministry continues, the ministry of married couples deserves acknowledgment and support. In their most personal and private decisions, husbands and wives share in the ministry of Christ—that is, they minister *as* Church. The whole Church, then, has a stake in the ministry of every couple.

Recent years have seen increased consciousness of the essential role parents play in the Church's educational ministry. More and more parishes are designing programs to help parents prepare their own children for the reception of the sacraments. Family-centered first reception of Eucharist and Reconciliation is becoming common. But couldn't parents' role become even more visible in the liturgy? They might, for instance, be appointed ministers of Communion when their child approaches the Lord's table for the first time. Or they might be designated the ordinary ministers of Baptism, with the priest or deacon serving as official witness as in Matrimony. (This would merely extend to parents a role already expected of them in emergency situations.)

Public liturgical roles for parents may seem startling, but parents have always been leaders of prayer. Besides traditional bedtime and meal prayers and the family rosary, many families are experimenting with a rich variety of new prayer forms—short Scripture services, song-prayers, blessing cup ceremonies.

Encouraging family prayer returns more of the Church to families, the "domestic Church." Parishes can support prayer-life in the home by seeking resources from publishers and from worship and family life commissions and making them available on the parish book rack or in the bulletin.

Church-related institutions can give practical support to marriage by paying married employees wages adequate for supporting a family. Finally, a parish can provide married people with a variety of volunteer services from baby-sitting during worship services to help with shopping, preparing meals and housework when a family is burdened with sickness or other distress.

The government could also give much greater support to marriage and family life. It could begin by eliminating tax penalties for married people. Direct financial aid to needy parents to enable home child care is better than publicly-funded day-care centers. Greater tax deductions for dependents and tax credits for alternatives to public education would also be an aid to people struggling to carry out parental responsibility.

Lest all the burden be put on the Church and the government, it must be remembered that everybody bears some responsibility for easing the burdens of married people and parents. This can be done first by a positive attitude toward married people who choose to have children. We can accept such people in our apartment complexes. We can avoid making married people feel guilty for staying home all day providing for the family, instead of being out in the world "doing something worthwhile." If we are employers, we can pay a family-supporting wage, provide time off for new fathers, and encourage employees to put the family first and the company second.

Conclusion

For centuries we have recognized the apostolic dimension of caring for orphans and neglected children, providing food for the poor and setting up health centers for the disadvantaged. This perception should make it easier to acknowledge marriage and parenting as ministry. In fact, to the degree that spouses and parents perform their ministry with wholehearted dedication, many of these other apostolic works and social services become less necessary.

For Reflection or Discussion

1) What images does the word *ministry* first bring to your mind? In what ways do you see yourself called to Christian ministry?

2) The author mentions seven aspects of Christian ministry. Drawing on your own experience describe how others have ministered to you in these ways; how you have ministered to others. Is there some need in a life close to yours that you could more effectively meet in one of these ways?

3) Read Matthew 25:34-40 and reflect on your response to the Lord's challenge—in the home, the parish and civic community, the world community. Do Jesus' words give more meaning and importance to the small, everyday services you perform for others?

4) From your own experience, cite examples of how other people's attitudes support—or fail to support—the ministry of married couples to each other, their children, the community. How and to whom can you give more support?

Partner-to-Partner Inventory

1) Do we perceive and experience our relationship with one another as a form of Christian ministry? How or how not?

2) In what ways has our relationship with one another strengthened our Christian faith? Do we have any suggestions about how in our relationship we can share and strengthen our faith even more?

3) How open are we to learn from one another about our strengths and weaknesses, our virtues and faults, and about how we can improve as persons and as a couple?

4) How much do we affirm and support each other by our attitude, our looks and gestures, our words and actions? In what ways do we cut each other down?

5) To what degree do we experience from one another the understanding, compassion and help that give healing, comfort and strength? How do we ease the burdens of life and enable each other to carry on with renewed energy and hope?

6) In what ways do we share ourselves, our relationship and our gifts with others so as to minister to their needs? To what degree have we achieved a balance between the one extreme of being too self-centered and closed in on ourselves, and the other extreme of being so involved with others that we neglect our primary responsibilities to one another?

For Couples Who Are Parents

1) Do we perceive our coparenting as an important ministry in our life, second only to our marriage? Or do we see parenting as an inconvenient distraction from the "really significant things" we would like to accomplish in life? What concrete indicators support our answer?

2) In what ways do we truly accept our children as the unique individuals they are and encourage them to become all they are called to become? In what ways do we put pressure on them to become what *we* have decided they ought to be?

3) How often and to what degree are we personally present to our children? In what concrete ways do we manifest this personal presence? Are there times when we are merely physically present?

4) Do both of us share equitably in ministering to the physical needs of our children? Or do we allow most of this burden to fall on the shoulders of only one of us? To what degree do we perform these physical tasks in a way that communicates our joy, our love and our interest in our children?

5) Do we consider ourselves the primary religious educators of our children? In what practical ways do we enact this role? How can we improve our efforts in the religious formation of our children?

PRAYER SERVICE

Ministry

Opening Prayer

Lord, you came to serve, not to be served. Through Baptism we have been called to share in your life of service. Help us in our marriage to grow in a spirit of mutual service, so that we may be a source of nurturing to one another, to our children and to those to whom we are sent. We pray this, Lord, in your name. Amen.

Scripture Reading

When the Son of man comes in his glory, escorted by all the angels, then he will take his seat on his throne of glory. All nations will be assembled before him and he will separate people one from another as the shepherd separates sheep from goats. He will place the sheep on his right hand and the goats on his left. Then the King will say to those on his right hand, "Come, you whom my Father has blessed, take as your heritage the kingdom prepared for you since the foundation of the world. For I was hungry and you gave me food, I was thirsty and you gave me drink, I was a stranger and you made me welcome, lacking clothes and you clothed me, sick and you visited me, in prison and you came to see me." Then the upright will say to him in reply, "Lord, when did we see you hungry and feed you, or thirsty and give you drink? When did we see you a stranger and make you welcome, lacking clothes and clothe you? When did we find you sick or in prison and go to see you?" And the King will answer, "In truth I tell you, in so far as you did this to one of the least of these brothers of mine, you did it to me." (Matthew 25:31-40)

79

Silent reflection

Sharing of thoughts on the reading

Litany

This Litany reflects three different moods: thanksgiving, penitence and resolution. Couples should pause between the sections and allow themselves to settle into the mood of the prayer.

For coming to serve us, and teaching us how to serve,
  We thank you, Lord.

For calling us to the ministry of marriage,
  We thank you, Lord.

For the nurturing we have experienced from one another,
  We thank you, Lord.

For the enrichment we have received from our children,
  We thank you, Lord.

For lack of sensitivity to one another's needs,
  Lord, have mercy.

For the times we have failed to minister to one another,
  Lord, have mercy.

For any unfairness and sexism in the distribution
of household tasks,
  Lord, have mercy.

For our lack of generosity in responding to the needs
of the poor and the sorrowing,
  Lord, have mercy.

We renew our commitment to serve one another
and our family in a spirit of generosity and joy,
  Lord, help us, we pray.

We will strive to base our service not on stereotypes
but rather on our mutual needs and desires,
>   Lord, help us, we pray.

We will respond more fully to Christ's call
to share ourselves and our resources with the needy,
>   Lord, help us, we pray.

The couple add further resolutions of their own.
>   Lord, help us, we pray.

Concluding Prayer

*(Refrain is recited together. The verses, taken from Psalm 23, can
be recited by either spouse.)*

Refrain: Yahweh is my shepherd, I lack nothing.

Yahweh is my shepherd, I lack nothing.
In grassy meadows he lets me lie.

By tranquil streams he leads me
>   to restore my spirit.
He guides me in paths of saving justice
>   as befits his name.

Refrain

Even were I to walk in a ravine as dark as death
I should fear no danger, for you are at my side.
Your staff and your crook are there to soothe me.

Refrain

You prepare a table for me
>   under the eyes of my enemies;
you anoint my head with oil;
>   my cup brims over.

Refrain

Kindness and faithful love pursue me
    every day of my life.
I make my home in the house of Yahweh
    for all time to come.

Refrain

Glory be to the Father,
and to the Son,
and to the Holy Spirit,
as it was in the beginning,
is now,
and ever shall be,
world without end. Amen.

Kiss *of* **Peace**

NOW THE HOUR has come
for the Son of man to be glorified.
In all truth I tell you,
unless a wheat grain falls into the earth and dies,
it remains only a single grain;
but if it dies
it yields a rich harvest.
Anyone who loves his life loses it;
anyone who hates his life in this world
will keep it for eternal life.
Whoever serves me, must follow me,
and my servant will be with me wherever I am.
If anyone serves me, my Father will honor him.
Now my soul is troubled.
What shall I say:
Father, save me from this hour?
But it is for this very reason that I have come to this hour.
Father, glorify your name! (John 12:23-28)

The Dying
and the Rising

*L*eaves fall away, blossoms bud forth. Seeds disappear, gardens grow. The charm of childhood is gone, the adult emerges. Humans die and, Christians believe, are raised up again.

All living is experienced as death and resurrection. The pain of loss is tempered by the hope and joy of new creation. Tears of sorrow give way to happy laughter.

Married life has its own rhythm of dying and rising. For the Christian this dimension can best be perceived in light of the death and resurrection of Jesus Christ.

Jesus Christ was one of us. Before his final victory over death, he experienced the full gamut of dyings and risings that mark the evolution of human life and growth. Born as an infant, he had to grow through childhood and adolescence into adulthood. "And Jesus increased in wisdom, in stature, and in favor with God and with people" (Luke 2:52). He had to surrender the beauty and advantages of one phase of life in order to grow into the strength and goodness of the next stage.

The biological aspects of the human growth process take place without our consent. But the kind of person we grow to be depends on our free choice to relinquish the security of the past and to build toward a new future in faith and love.

In the Gospels Jesus moves with vision into the future. At age 12 he broke, though briefly, from dependence on his parents and engaged in dialogue with the doctors in the Temple. In his adulthood he left behind the safe anonymity of life in Nazareth and embarked on a ministry as itinerant preacher and healer that brought him mixed notoriety. As the end of his life drew near, "he resolutely turned his face toward Jerusalem" (Luke 9:51), where his ministry culminated on Calvary.

The dyings and risings of Jesus are also apparent in his relationships with people. In the midst of his ministry "many of his disciples went away and accompanied him no more" (John 6:66). Judas betrayed him and committed suicide. Peter denied him and came back. These lapses of loyalty did not make Jesus cynical or bitter, but revealed new dimensions of his forgiving love.

Finally, Jesus was crucified as a criminal and a blasphemer. Amidst hostility, he prayed for his enemies. Despite seeming defeat he entrusted himself to the hands of God, his Father. Ultimately, the darkness of Good Friday yielded to the glory of Easter Sunday and Jesus, through death, was tranformed with the newness of risen life to become the source of rebirth for all humanity.

Our Call to Die and to Rise

Through Baptism Christians participate in the death and resurrection of Christ.

> You cannot have forgotten that all of us, when we were baptized into Christ Jesus, were baptized into his death. So by our baptism into his death we were buried with him, so that as Christ was raised from the dead by the Father's glorious power, we too should begin living a new life. (Romans 6:3-4)

Water, the symbol used in Baptism, is a sign of both death and life. Through Baptism we die to sinfulness. Receiving the grace of Christ, we become like him and live in the Spirit of his truth and love. But this baptismal dying and rising is not a once and for all event. The Christian is called to die a little more each day to disbelief, alienation, egoism, injustice, in order to live more fully in communion with Christ and with genuine, loving concern for others. At the end of life's journey we embrace death as a sign of our trust in God, in order to share fully in Christ's risen life. Through our ultimate participation in the death and resurrection of Christ we achieve unity with God and one another.

Dying and Rising in Marriage

In marriage the Christian couple live out their baptismal call by growing in relationship to each other. They share Christ's death and resurrection by working through all the dyings and risings required for two to become one. In this way they make visible the love with which Christ died and rose from the dead.

To make this reality concrete and practical, we will examine some of the dyings and risings that are an integral part of the marital relationship.

1) *Dying to a self-protective shell, rising to marital communion.* We tend to protect our inner selves from people. If others get to know us, they might not accept us. If we go out to them in love, they may reject us.

In order for spouses to grow in union with one another, they must be willing to shed their protective shells. They need to take off the masks, put aside the defensive games people play, and stand naked before each other—psychologically and spiritually as well as physically. Putting aside their fears and embarrassments, they allow the other to know them as they are, with their beauty and defects, their strengths and weaknesses. They take the risk of being misunderstood in order to receive understanding. They take the chance of being hurt in order to taste the joy of being appreciated. They risk being rejected in their nakedness in order to be accepted in the total embrace of love. Dying to the barriers that can keep them at a safe distance from each other, they emerge enriched in intimacy and communion.

2) *Dying to other possible sexual unions, rising to exclusive permanent relationship.* Marital union involves turning aside from all other conceivable marriages and possible partners in order to build a unique and lasting relationship with one person. One renounces other sexual liaisons and love affairs in order to find intimacy, exclusivity and fidelity in married life. The heart of marital chastity is rooted in the decision that a spouse makes to forego the pleasure of other beds in order to channel sexual energies toward creating a life of mutually enriching, committed love.

3) *Dying to illusions, rising to realistic possibilities.* People enter into marriage with a variety of dreams and expectations about their spouse and the life that they will build together. As dream worlds give way to the hard realities of life, a couple must die to their illusions and false expectations. Living in commitment to each other is not the same thing as dating under selective circumstances. One's spouse looks different in day-to-day routine than on a moonlit evening.

During periods of disillusionment a couple is challenged to let go of the unreal and to dedicate themselves to making the most of the realistic opportunities that their particular marriage affords. They put aside idealized images of one another so as to accept and appreciate what is good and to confront creatively what is difficult in each other. They cease to long unrealistically for a life free from financial struggles, relational tensions and personal conflicts. Instead they work through their problems within the realistic context of their situation. They compromise their dreams in order to build a life of stability and harmony.

4) *Dying to alienation and estrangement, rising to reconciliation and deepened bonds.* In the day-to-day interactions that make up married life it is inevitable that misunderstandings, hurt feelings and harsh words occur at least occasionally. After such occurrences, people are sometimes tempted to withdraw from one

another, keep a safe distance and maybe even sulk in silence. Those who swallow their pride can break down any walls of resentment that have been built up and take the first step toward bridging gaps. In this way difficulties that arise can become an occasion for a new closeness sealed by sorrow, forgiveness and sensitive healing.

5) *Dying to other priorities, rising to the foremost priority.* One of the painful difficulties of human life is that there are countless things we would like to accomplish, with a very limited amount of time and energy. Hence we must choose among the many goods and values that lie before us.

In married life we find ourselves pulled in a number of directions. We want a good relationship with our spouse. Duties, chores and jobs also demand attention. We would like to have more money, get ahead professionally, maybe even make a name for ourselves. We need to cultivate other friends; we would like to get along socially. Needy people look to us for help. There are times when we want to be alone, to read, to listen to music. We each have hobbies we like to pursue and favorite programs and sports events we enjoy.

How do we balance all of our responsibilities and interests with the commitment to create a happy marriage? We need to set priorities. If the first value in our life is building a good marital relationship, we will see to it that our other goals and pursuits serve the interest of the marriage, rather than endanger it. This sometimes entails surrendering certain worthwhile involvements so as to keep our spouse in the order of first importance.

6) *Dying to independence, rising to cooperation.* Most of us yearn—at least sometimes—to be independent and free from accountability. In marriage the happiness and destiny of another are tied to our own course of action. Therefore, we must die to the tendency to consider only ourselves in making personal decisions—choice of employment, major expenditures, the time we will arrive home for dinner. The needs, convenience and desires of a spouse must be considered even in quite personal matters when they affect the well-being of the partner. By

conquering this kind of self-centeredness, we grow in sensitive awareness of each other.

7) *Dying to certain stages in marriage, rising to new horizons.* Life never stands still. We can never recapture the past in exactly the same way. As we grow older together, we change in looks, vitality and tastes. If we have children, we share in the dyings and risings that comprise their journey to adulthood.

A life-style suitable to an earlier stage of our marriage may be out of place in our lives today. We must die to former phases in our marital relationship, so that we might be able to accept each other anew, embrace the present reality of our married lives, and build toward the promise of the unseen future.

8) *Dying to mortal life, rising to eternal life.* All humans share the one certain prospect of earthly existence: death. The mystery of dying invokes in most of us a mixture of fear and sadness, hope and anticipation. We embrace life, knowing it will lead to death. We accept death, believing it will lead to life.

When we are happily married, the picture of death becomes more complicated. Because our lives have become intertwined in a unique way, our deaths become interconnected. The thought of our own death becomes more painful when we must consider what happens to a surviving spouse and children. A spouse's death causes a kind of dying in the one who survives.

From the moment we begin to grow in love, we know the day will come when death will physically set us apart. The more our involvement binds us together, the more painful becomes the prospect of separation in death. Yet we do not hold back. We dare give of ourselves to one another, believing and trusting that even the sorrow of death will deepen our love and bring new life both to the one who dies and to the ones who remain behind.

Conclusion

Unless the seed falls into the earth and dies, it remains but an isolated seed. If it dies, it yields a rich harvest. The ongoing newness of life in marriage is born of the discipline and sacrifice found in certain forms of self-renunciation. By dying to self-centeredness, fear and, ultimately, to earthly life itself, a couple can rise to new heights of authentic love, union and enrichment.

For Reflection or Discussion

1) What meaning does the death and resurrection of Christ have for you?

2) From your own experience, can you recall exciting new beginnings that entailed a measure of loss, occasions where you had to leave something behind to move on to something better? Can you also recall real and painful losses which brought you new insight, hope or opportunity?

3) The author describes eight "dyings and risings" in marriage. How many of these have figured into your own primary relationships? Can you describe others?

4) Can you pinpoint in your life right now any area of resistance to "dying"? What opportunities for "resurrection" can you imagine?

Partner-to-Partner Inventory

1) How deeply do we believe in the resurrection of Jesus? How firm is our faith that after death we too will pass into risen life?

2) How much do these beliefs enable us to trust that from the various dyings in our marriage, growth and new life can emerge?

3) To what degree have we died to: a) self-centeredness; b) self-protective shells that prevent closer intimacy; c) sexist stereotypes?

4) How well have we adjusted to transitions in our life and our relationship?

5) Are there any things from the past to which we need to die in order to grow and to live the present more fully?

6) Have we discussed and faced the fact that some day one of us will die and most probably leave the other behind? Have we accepted this reality and made realistic preparations for it?

7) Have we died to expressions of parenting that were appropriate when our children were younger, but have now become a barrier to growth? How well have we adjusted to new ways of relating to them in their present stage of development?

PRAYER SERVICE

Dying and Rising

An attractive bowl of water and a towel should be readied for this service.

Opening Prayer

Lord Jesus, you accepted death out of love for us. Through your dying you passed into risen life. Help us to die to all that obstructs growing maturity and intimacy in our relationship, so that we may achieve the fullness of life to which you call us. We pray this, Lord, in your name. Amen.

Scripture Reading

Make your own the mind of Christ Jesus:

Who, being in the form of God,
did not count equality with God
something to be grasped.

But he emptied himself,
taking the form of a slave,
becoming as human beings are;
and being in every way like a human being,
he was humbler yet,
even to accepting death, death on a cross.

And for this God raised him high,
and gave him the name
which is above all other names;

so that all beings
in the heavens, on earth and in the underworld,

93

should bend the knee at the name of Jesus

and that every tongue should acknowledge
Jesus Christ as Lord,
to the glory of God the Father. (Philippians 2:5-11)

Silent reflection

Sharing of thoughts on the reading

Litany

This Litany reflects three different moods: thanksgiving, penitence and resolution. Couples should pause between the sections and allow themselves to settle into the mood of the prayer.

For your death and resurrection,
>We thank you, Lord.

For the hope you give us in difficult times,
>We thank you, Lord.

For the new life you have enabled us to achieve
through the various dyings in our relationship,
>We thank you, Lord.

For the risen life we hope to receive after death,
>We thank you, Lord.

For our lack of trust and hope,
>Lord, have mercy.

For our failure to die to self-centeredness and possessiveness,
>Lord, have mercy.

For any unhealthy clinging to the past,
>Lord, have mercy.

For our reluctance to accept and adapt to necessary changes,
>Lord, have mercy.

We resolve to grow in faith
that the Lord will be with us in all our futures,
and will lead us through any dark valleys
to green pastures,
> Lord, help us, we pray.

We will strive to support each other's personal growth
and development,
and to make any adjustments such growth necessitates,
> Lord, help us, we pray.

We will make an effort to be understanding
and compassionate toward one another
as we journey through the various passages
of adulthood.
> Lord, help us, we pray.

The couple add further resolutions of their own.
> Lord, help us, we pray.

Water Rite

Each partner places her or his hands into the bowl of water, praying spontaneously or saying these words:

In Baptism I was plunged into the waters and emerged with new life. Lord, help me to live out my baptismal commitment by being willing to share more fully in your death and resurrection.

The hands are then raised out of the water. The other partner dries them.

Concluding Prayer

Refrain is recited together. The verses, taken from Ecclesiastes 3:1-7, may be recited by either spouse.

Refrain: Unless a wheat grain falls into the earth and dies,
it remains only a single grain;
but if it dies
it yields a rich harvest. (John 12:24)

There is a season for everything, a time for every occupation under heaven....

Refrain

A time for giving birth,
a time for dying;
a time for planting,
a time for uprooting what has been planted.

Refrain

A time for killing,
a time for healing;
a time for knocking down,
a time for building.

Refrain

A time for tears,
a time for laughter;
a time for mourning,
a time for dancing.

Refrain

A time for throwing stones away,
a time for gathering them;
a time for embracing,
a time to refrain from embracing.

Refrain

A time for searching,
a time for losing;
a time for keeping,
a time for discarding.

Refrain

A time for tearing,
a time for sewing;
a time for keeping silent,
a time for speaking. (Ecclesiastes 3:1-7)

Refrain

Glory be to the Father
and to the Son,
and to the Holy Spirit,
as it was in the beginning,
is now,
and ever shall be,
world without end. Amen.

Kiss of Peace

FOR THE TRADITION I received from the Lord and also handed on to you is that on the night he was betrayed, the Lord Jesus took some bread, and after he had given thanks, he broke it, and he said, "This is my body, which is for you; do this in remembrance of me." And in the same way, with the cup after supper, saying, "This cup is the new covenant in my blood. Whenever you drink it, do this as a memorial of me." Whenever you eat this bread, then, and drink this cup, you are proclaiming the Lord's death until he comes. (1 Corinthians 11:23-26)

S I X

Bread Broken,
Body Given

Wherever there is bread, there is
a sacrificial body behind it. Somebody has labored long hours in
the field, tilling the soil, planting the seed and reaping the harvest
of wheat. Somebody stood by the hot bakery ovens transforming
dough into loaves of bread. And somebody paid the cost to bring
bread to the table.

Wherever a meal is served there is body-presence. It may be
the mechanical presence of a fast-foods attendant punching keys
as the order is called out, or the professional presence of a waiter
at pains to explain the menu specials, or the intimate presence
manifested in a dinner for two or in a family celebration.

Bread and body: the two are intimately connected. Without
bread we would starve and die; without human presence, our lives
would be barren. We need other people around us to alleviate our
aloneness. Mere physical presence is not enough. We yearn for
others who are *personally* present to us, others who acknowledge
our existence and importance, who respond to us and manifest
interest and concern.

In the belief of most Christian traditions, bread and body
come together perfectly in Eucharist. The bread becomes the body

of Christ present to us in personal concern and love. The body of Christ becomes the bread offered to us in companionship for the enrichment of our lives. At every Eucharist Christ is the body "behind" the bread. He is the body-person present in the breaking of the bread at the meal of the New Covenant.

Married life, like Eucharist, is centered around the sharing of bread and the giving of one's body. In the breaking of their bread and the giving of their bodies, the married couple is a sign of Christ's body-gift to us in the Eucharist.

To examine the Eucharistic dimension of Christian marriage, we will first reflect on Christ's gift of self in Eucharist. We can then explore how his gift is paralleled in the shared food and the bodily expression of love in marriage.

The Eucharist

In his ministry Christ proclaimed his Word and gave of his body in healing touch. On occasion he fed the hungry with physical bread. When he did so, he made clear that any physical bread he gave was a sign of the deeper gift of the bread of himself (see John 6:1-15, 22-71).

His word and his healing led to difficulties with some of the authorities. Because of what he stood for and the way he ministered, Jesus was rejected and crucified. To show that his death, like his life, was a gift freely given for us, he celebrated a special meal with his disciples the night before he died. He took some bread, gave thanks, broke it and gave it to them, saying, "This is my body given for you..." (Luke 22:19). Then taking the cup of wine he gave it to them saying, "Drink from this, all of you, for this is my blood, the blood of the covenant, poured out for many for the forgiveness of sins" (Matthew 26:27-28).

In the Eucharist the crucified and risen Christ continues to give us the gift of himself, with the same love with which he died for us. The bread and wine he gives are signs of the gift of his own person to us. Bread and wine alone have no redemptive value. They would be cheap substitutes for the costly and sacrificial gift of self. Not by bread alone do humans live (see Matthew 4:4).

Christ's personal communication of himself in covenant and friendship enriches and transforms us. In Eucharist we affirm that Christ loves us, that he is with us and for us. He gives himself as security for our pilgrimage through a very unstable world. He provides us with happiness even in the midst of sadness, hope even in the midst of despair.

'Real Presence' in Marriage

Eucharist is a model for Christian marriage. As Eucharist has personal value for Christians because it involves Christ's gift of himself in shared bread and wine, so marriage has personal value for the couple because it involves the self-gift of wife and husband to each other in shared daily life.

In the context of their life together the couple give many things to each other: food and drink, housing, clothes and a variety of articles that provide convenience, comfort and entertainment. They also perform many services on behalf of one another. The value that things and actions have for making the couple happier and more deeply in love depends on one factor: Are the things given and the actions performed *signs* of the ongoing gift of self to one another? Or less costly *substitutes*?

One might provide expensive things (jewelry, excursions, automobiles), hoping these might take the place of the costly gift of one's whole self for the other. One spouse might be busy about many things (household chores, home improvement, taking care of the children) as a way of escaping intimate personal presence to the other. When the things we give and do for another are substitutes rather than signs of the deeper gift of ourselves to our spouse, they fail to bring us together in deeper communion. Substitutes may set us even further apart. Marriages cannot be built on the giving of things and the bustle of activity. Happiness, personal transformation, redemption in marriage are experienced in the sacrificial gift of body-person to body-person.

101

Married couples celebrate the gift of themselves in two central places: at the *table* where they break bread and in the *bed* where they give their bodies to one another. There marriage bears a parallel with the breaking of bread and the giving of Christ's body in the Eucharist.

At table the couple share food and drink and themselves as the Lord does at Eucharist. Through the shared meal they communicate more deeply of themselves to each other; they enter into more intimate personal communion with one another.

In the sexual expression of love the couple give their bodies to one another as Jesus gives his in the Eucharist. Through the mutual giving they dwell more deeply in one another and become more fully one, not only in a physical sense but also in the personal dimension of their being.

Just as the Eucharist unites us with Christ in proportion to the love for Christ we manifest throughout our lives, so too shared table and bed enrich a marital relationship in proportion to the love manifested in every aspect of our lives. If our meals are to enhance our personal communion with our spouse, the sharing of food must be a sign of the deeper sharing of ourselves with each other. This presupposes intimate communication not only at mealtime but throughout our lives together. If sexual intercourse is to unite us more deeply as total persons, it must express the commitment to be for each other that we daily demonstrate in countless ways.

The Table

In coming together at the same table, the couple acknowledge two basic needs of human living: the need for food and the need for companionship. They meet at the table in loving sacrifice for the mutual satisfaction of these two basic hungers.

The food has cost them its price: employment, money, time to prepare and serve the meal. Together they have sacrificed. Together they share the reward: the assuagement of physical hunger.

102

But food alone, even when eaten at the same table, is only food. As such, it has only physical power, the power to provide bodily nourishment. The deeper hunger for companionship and personal communion is satisfied to the degree that the meal is an expression of their desire to become more united in mind and heart. A meal with such personal significance nourishes the marital covenant and strengthens family community. In order for a meal to have such power, married people must attend to several principles:

1) *Sharing a family meal together on a regular basis is a foremost priority.* This first involves an attitude, a belief in the importance and unitive power of a shared meal. It also involves sacrificing other priorities and coordinating schedules—a difficult challenge in an age where many couples both work and children are involved in numerous activities. Too easily the family dining room gives way to the kitchen cafeteria and a tremendous opportunity for family members to know and be close to one another is lost.

With effort, communication and careful planning we can preserve a regular schedule of family meals. Certain days and times can be agreed upon. Where different work shifts make a shared evening meal an impossibility, the morning or noon meal might become the time for family gathering.

2) *Some kind of psychological preparation is necessary.* The moments immediately prior to meals are not the time to become preoccupied with financial worries and other family problems. Nor is it the time to begin marital disputes. It is a time for sensitivity, gentleness and celebration of the love that binds us together.

The weekday evening meal can be particularly problematic. The critical moment when fatigued breadwinners arrive home to cope with tired children and boiling pots promises little joy at the table. Couples need to organize the day to allow at least a few "quiet" moments to extend civilities, relax tensions and recover some degree of normalcy after a long and trying day.

3) *All family members are responsible for shared meals.*

103

Shopping, food preparation, cooking, serving and cleanup need not be one person's sole and perennial burden. Couples can share these chores. At a very early age children can learn to set the table, remove their own dishes and gradually make their own creative contributions to the preparation of the food. If all family members share these chores with generosity and kindness, even the work can become fun and provide an opportunity for communication.

4) *A pleasant atmosphere of interest and concern for one another at table is a conscious creation.* Television distracts attention from people; so do phone calls and small children who leave their place and run around during meals. The TV can be silenced and phone calls returned. When very young children become restless they can be excused. Children can learn not to interrupt the conversation of others—and they learn best by example. Loud noises and other circus-like activity need not be permitted. Being on time for meals and making an effort to be cheerfully present to one another can normally be expected at the family table.

5) *The meal is a good time for brief family prayer.* Especially as children grow up, the meal may be the one time the family is gathered together. It provides a good opportunity for shared prayer before and/or after the meal. This prayer, in turn, helps focus on the deeper significance of the meal and contributes to its unifying effect.

6) *Couples with children need to celebrate some meals alone.* It is very important for parents to create opportunities when they can be together without the children, when they can celebrate with food and drink the growth of their own personal relationship. This doesn't happen automatically. It usually involves planning ahead, making the time and setting aside funds that could easily be used for other purposes. Sometimes the couple may enjoy these meals in a restaurant. At other times the couple may wish a late evening candlelight supper at home.

The Bed

Sexual expression is the most intimate symbolic way in which a couple show their love for one another. As Christians, we can counterbalance the negative attitudes toward sexuality that have arisen in many cultures and in some religious circles over the centuries if we perceive marital intercourse in the context of Eucharist. From this perspective, three significant insights emerge.

1) *Both Eucharist and sexual intercourse involve the giving and receiving of the human body in a life-giving way.* The gift of another's body enriches our personhood because we are embodied persons. If anything is to touch and affect our person, it must touch and affect our body. Whatever touches and affects our body, touches and affects our personhood. We are, after all, body-person, *not* body *and* person.

When God wished to touch our personhood in the fullest way possible, the Word of God became flesh, became human body. Through the body-person of Christ, God touches embodied humanity. In the Eucharistic bread and wine Christ gives us his body and enters into communion with our body-person. Through this visible, tangible, sacramental contact with Christ we receive joy and comfort, and some of our deeper yearnings for love and union are satisfied.

In marriage we give of ourselves to each other in genital and bodily expression. Through our intimate embraces we touch the inner being of each other. We heal, enrich and empower one another—psychologically and spiritually as well as physically. On a profoundly personal level we bring each other comfort, happiness and a deep sense of well-being.

2) *Both Eucharist and intercourse are "now" and "not yet."* Both are experiences of union in the present moment; both are a promise of unity still to come. We experience in Eucharist the joy of Christ's presence now, and yet we become acutely aware of the incompleteness of our union with Christ, of the distance that continues to separate us. Through the joy and the pain we grow toward greater union.

In sexual intercourse we experience the pleasure (sometimes ecstatic) of our intimacy with one another. Even when the closeness is intense and exhilarating, however, we can be aware of the distance between us. Our yearning for complete communion is never satisfied. There always remain part of me and part of you that are beyond grasp. Through the joy and the pain we can, however, grow in life-giving union.

3) *Both Eucharist and intercourse draw us to God.* Just as our desire for Eucharist is an expression of our longing for communion with the Divine, so too our yearning for sexual expression of love with our spouse cannot be isolated from our passion for transcendent union with God. In the sacrament of marriage God communicates to us through the love we express for one another. In responding to our spouse's love we are responding to God's manifestation of love. In reaching out for intimacy with one another, we are reaching out for intimacy with the Transcendent One. Sexual desire for our spouse is evidence of our insatiable longing for personal communion that can find total satisfaction only in God. When sexual intercourse is an authentic expression of love for each other, it is always grace-giving; that is, it leads to deeper personal union not only with our spouse but also with our God.

From these insights several practical implications can be drawn.

1) *Marital intercourse is a gift, not a duty.* We give ourselves freely and gratuitously in genital expression as a sign of our mutual love and our mutual desire to please and enrich each other. The sign is distorted when sexual intercourse in marriage is reduced to a matter of obligation — "to render the debt," as some of the old moral theology books unfortunately spoke of it. It was even worse when that obligation was primarily applied to women.

Distortion also occurs when sexual intercourse becomes an object of barter. "I work so hard all day; the least you can do is reward me in bed." "If you don't give in, I'll get back at you." "Because you have displeased me, I'll refuse you." If marital intercourse for the Christian is a sacramental reflection of Christ's gracious and grace-filled gift of himself in love, it cannot be demanded or performed reluctantly under pressure. The decision to express or not express ourselves in a genital way should be agreed upon with mutual freedom, sensitivity to one another and gracious generosity.

2) *Sexual intercourse is not a solution to marital problems; a long-term satisfying sex life in marriage presupposes a sound relationship.* At the very root of our desire for sexual expression is our longing for personal communion, acceptance and love. If this mutual giving and acceptance on a personal level is lacking in our lives, it will be absent in our sexual expression. Such absence renders sexual intercourse incapable of satisfying our deepest needs for personal union and for a sense of belonging and being loved.

If, on the other hand, we are seriously striving to grow in love and union in all the other aspects of our married life, to that degree sexual intercourse will be enhanced with personal meaning. When sexual intercourse has this meaning, it helps strengthen the marital relationship in its deepest dimensions. it empowers the couple to live out the total self-giving they have expressed in bed.

3) *Sexual intercourse is life-giving for the couple and only subsequently for children.* While sexual relations are intimately associated with conception, it is important that this fact not obscure the deep connection between intercourse and the life of the marital relationship. Only a very small percentage of sexual encounters produce children. All of them can enrich the sensitivity and compassion, love and generosity of the couple. Enriching a couple's relationship with each other enhances their relationship with their children and warms the home's atmosphere. Hence it contributes to the ongoing giving of life to children.

4) *Marital chastity involves manifesting in sexual expression those personal qualities that sacramentalize Christ's eucharistic love.* In determining what is chaste or unchaste in the marital expression of sexual intimacy, most of the emphasis has usually

been placed on what is biologically "according to nature." While biological considerations are important, they are by themselves insufficient in defining the Christian virtue of marital chastity. If sexual love in marriage is to be a sign of Christ's love, then the psychological and spiritual quality of genital intimacy takes on paramount significance.

What is truly unchaste in bed is exploitation, self-centeredness, manipulation, insensitivity and sexism. Marital chastity on the other hand, reflects commitment, fidelity, respect for the dignity and otherness of a spouse. It involves concern, caring, gentleness and the willingness to communicate openly about mutual needs and desires, likes and dislikes in the area of sexual love. A chaste couple manifest in their genital intimacy trust in each other, enjoyment of one another's body, a sense of humor and play.

5) *Marital intercourse is a means, not an obstacle, to growth in our union with God and Christ.* This would seem a rather obvious conclusion from all that has preceded. The past history of theology, however, gives witness to how difficult it has been to apply to sexual intercourse the many beautiful insights associated with the sacrament of marriage. Some of the Church Fathers thought it impossible for a couple to engage in sexual intercourse without committing venial sin. Others saw a conflict between sexual relations and a prayer life. While these opinions are not officially espoused, negative feelings still lurk deep in the psyche. Do we really believe that a couple can grow in holiness *through* their sexual expression of love—not in spite of it? Do we accept the fact that sexual intercourse can be one of the most sacramental moments in living the sacrament of marriage?

6) *Sex in marriage provides an important insight into the God whose love for humans is described in wife-husband imagery.* Human beings are created in the image and likeness of God. They are created as sexual beings. Sexuality and the ability to love in a sexual way come from God. Through their experience of genitally expressed love—the pleasure, the play, the humor, the "foolishness," the earthiness, the ecstatic moments—a couple can

reflect on the God who stands behind it all. This is our God: a God of "foolishness," a God so down to earth as to become involved forever in the human situation in and through Jesus Christ.

Conclusion

In the Eucharist we grow in union with Christ through the giving and receiving of bread and wine, the giving and receiving of Christ's body and blood. In marriage we grow in union with one another in the sharing of our food and drink and in the mutual giving and receiving of our bodies in the sexual expression of love.

Since love in marriage is a sign of Christ's love for us, we find Christ in our shared meals and our sexual encounters. These, in turn, enable us more deeply to experience Christ and one another in our shared celebration of Eucharist. How well we accomplish all this depends, of course, on the depth of our commitment to Christ and to one another.

For Reflection or Discussion

1) How would you explain Eucharist to someone totally unfamiliar with the concept? Would the imagery you use be personal and intimate (meal, body-presence, self-gift) or more formal (sacrifice, adoration, Real Presence)?

2) To what extent do you see sharing bread and bed as holy? Can you relate these activities to the Eucharist as the author does?

3) Does your experience of the family meal conform to your need for intimate personal communion? What factors contribute or detract from this sense? What can you do to enhance the experience?

4) What principles would you add to the author's treatment of the family meal? What insights or practical applications would you add to his treatment of marital intercourse?

Partner-to-Partner Inventory

1) What place does the celebration of the Eucharist have in our life of Christian faith? What place does it have in our relationship? Is the meaning of Eucharist for us limited to an hour on Sunday, or does it shape and direct the way we daily relate to each other?

2) To what degree are the things that we do for each other and give to one another *signs* of the deeper gift of self? Are there any ways in which these are used as mere *substitutes* for the gift of oneself to the other?

3) What role did the sharing of food and drink play in our courtship? What role does it have today in our relationship?

4) How important is it to us to have a regularly scheduled family meal? Why or why not?

5) What are some of the things we do that have helped the family meal to be a time of sharing? What have been some obstacles? Are there any concrete steps we can take to shape the family meal into an even more pleasant, enriching experience?

6) What are the positive (or wholesome) elements in our views of sexuality? Does either of us view sexuality in any negative ways?

7) How does sexuality fit into our views of God and how we relate to God? Does the relationship with God have anything to do with the experience of sexuality?

8) In what ways does our sexual expression of love satisfy each of us? In what ways does it leave either one of us dissatisfied? In what ways would either of us like to see our sex life improved?

Eucharistic Giving

Place a loaf of bread on a table.

Opening Prayer

Lord, Jesus, at every Eucharist you do sacramentally what you did at the Last Supper. You take bread and wine and, in giving them to us, you give us the gift of yourself in total friendship and love. Help us to give generously of ourselves to each other, so that in the giving and the receiving we may ever discover your presence. We pray this, Lord, in your name. Amen.

Scripture Reading

> I am the bread of life.
> Your fathers ate manna in the desert
> and they are dead;
> but this is the bread which comes down from heaven,
> so that a person may eat it and not die.
> I am the living bread which has come down from heaven.
> Anyone who eats this bread will live for ever;
> and the bread that I shall give
> is my flesh, for the life of the world. (John 6:48-51)

Silent reflection

Sharing of thoughts on the reading

Litany

This Litany reflects three different moods: thanksgiving, penitence and resolution. Couples should pause between the sections and allow themselves to settle into the mood of the prayer.

For the gift of yourself in Eucharist,
> We thank you, Lord.

For enabling us to be gift for one another,
> We thank you, Lord.

For all the family meals that have brought us
closer together,
> We thank you, Lord.

For the gift of ourselves in sexual love,
> We thank you, Lord.

For the times when we lacked gratitude for the gift
of Eucharist,
> Lord, have mercy.

For any way in which we failed to give of ourselves
to one another,
> Lord, have mercy.

For our inadequacies in making the family meal
an enriching and pleasant experience,
> Lord, have mercy.

For any lack of sensitivity, understanding and generosity
in the sexual expression of love,
> Lord, have mercy.

We will try to express more fully Christ's eucharistic love
in our love for one another,
> Lord, help us, we pray.

The couple add further resolutions of their own.
    Lord, help us, we pray.

Breaking of the Bread

In turn, each partner takes the loaf of bread, breaks a piece and gives it to the other, with these or similar words:

    I share this bread with you as a sign of renewed commitment to be with you and for you always.

Concluding Prayer

Refrain is recited together. The verses, taken from Psalm 104, may be recited by either spouse.

Refrain: Bless Yahweh, my soul,
Yahweh, my God, how great you are! (104:1)

In the ravines you opened up springs,
running down between the mountains,
supplying water for all the wild beasts;
the wild asses quench their thirst,
on their banks the birds of the air make their nests,
they sing among the leaves.

Refrain

From your high halls you water the mountains,
satisfying the earth with the fruit of your works:
for cattle you make the grass grow,
and for people the plants they need,
to bring forth food from the earth,
and wine to cheer people's hearts,
oil to make their faces glow,
food to make them sturdy of heart.

Refrain

They all depend upon you,
to feed them when they need it.
You provide the food they gather,
your open hand gives them their fill.

Refrain

Turn away your face and they panic;
take back their breath and they die
and revert to dust.
Send out your breath and life begins;
you renew the face of the earth.

Refrain

I shall sing to Yahweh all my life,
make music for my God as long as I live.

Refrain

Kiss of Peace

As a body is one though it has many parts, and all the parts of the body, though many, are one body, so also Christ. For in one Spirit we were all baptized into one body, whether Jews or Greeks, slaves or free persons, and we were all given to drink of one Spirit.

(1 Corinthians 12:12-13 NAB)

SEVEN

The Family
as Domestic Church

*T*he word *church* brings many images to mind: the building with its steeple and cross, the hierarchy with their miters and croziers, the parish with its priests and people. How often would the family assembled around the hearth or gathered about the table immediately come to mind among the images ordinarily associated with *church*?

One of the significant accomplishments of the bishops at the Second Vatican Council is that they brought together the two concepts, family and Church. As already noted in our discussion of marriage as ministry, the bishops described the family as "the domestic Church."

In this chapter we will first explain why it is appropriate to call the family the domestic Church. We will then indicate practical ways in which the family can grow as Church.

Domestic Church

To some it might seem strange to call the family a Church. If we reflect on the meaning of *church*, however, and examine what constitutes a truly Christian family, we can readily see that the family contains the most significant characteristics essential to being a Christian Church.

1) *The Church is the people of God, gathered together by the Spirit.* It is a community of those who have been baptized into life with the crucified and risen Christ. This community explicitly and consciously believes in Christ as the Word of God enfleshed, as the one who has redeemed us. For the Christian, Jesus Christ is the way, the truth and the life. He leads us to the God whom he calls *Abba*, Father.

The family is the smallest unit of this people called together by the Spirit. The Christian family is united not only by ties of blood, but also by the common bond of baptism into Christ. Family members share with one another their faith and love of Christ. Together they turn to him in prayer. In good times they give thanks and praise. In bad times they are held together by a common hope and trust.

2) *The Church is a community of persons committed to be disciples of Jesus Christ.* This means they strive to be influenced in their choices and their actions by personal relationship with Christ. They try to accept his value system and to translate his teaching into their daily lives.

The family is the first arena in which we live—or fail to live—the Gospel. It is, if you will, the primary testing ground for authentic Christian discipleship. It is in the intimate surroundings of family life that we are daily challenged to enflesh the values of Christ in the way we treat one another. Do we put persons before things? Do we accept a simple life-style? Do we really believe that it is better to serve than to be served?

3) *The Church shares in the mission of Christ.* At the very center of this mission is the call to promote the Kingdom of God.

If the Kingdom of God is to be spread, this must be done first in the home. The Christian family has the foremost responsibility of creating within itself relationships built on love and forgiveness, peace and justice, compassion and service. Furthering the reign of God in its own midst enables the family to promote God's Kingdom in the wider community.

4) *The Church is a people called to grow in communion with one another.* Such growth demands that Church members acknowledge when anything divides them and work to remove all obstacles to unity. The Church is always in need of purification and reform, always called to conversion and reconciliation.

Achieving deeper unity and greater intimacy is a lifelong challenge for every family. This demands celebrating the unity we have already achieved, as well as facing the ways in which we fail to share true community and intimacy. In the context of living closely together in the family, we are challenged to face our shortcomings and weaknesses as well as our virtues and strengths. We learn to say, "I am sorry," "I forgive." We discover that, with goodwill, we can often work through the hurts and tears to the joy and security of an even stronger bond.

5) *The Church is a people who gather around the communion table to break bread and share the cup in memory of the Lord.* This gathering is meant to be the centerpiece of Christian life. Having partaken of the Eucharist, Church members are called to go forth and do as Christ does: to share with others their bread, their cup, the gift of themselves in healing love.

The central act of worship for the Christian family is also the Eucharist. The family celebrates its Christian faith, especially on the Sabbath, by partaking of Communion. This experience enables the family to be aware of the communion dimensions of their own family meal. Just as the shared Eucharist has power to unify us in faith and love, so too the shared family meal can help us grow in understanding, concern and intimacy with one another. Just as participation in the Eucharist inspires us to go forth and share our bread, so too the family meal can sensitize us to one another in the many other moments that constitute the rhythm of our daily lives.

6) *The Church is a pilgrim people.* The bishops at the Second Vatican Council applied this striking image. The Church is not a static reality, but a people called to the dynamic process of growth and life. The Church is on a journey. It never fulfills its dream or reaches its destination this side of human history.

The family, too, is on a pilgrimage. It comes into being by the dynamic yes that the couple proclaims at the advent of each new member. It is on a journey that leads it through valleys and hills, through hard times and good. The family, like the Church, never reaches its full potential this side of the grave. But, with mutual support and encouragement, family members plod on, working toward that greater unity and love which beckons them.

These, then, are some of the characteristics that are essential to the notion of Christian Church. Their presence in a family constitute that family as a domestic Church. Indeed, families are the basic units of the total Church. Without Christian families, there simply would be no Christian Church.

The preceding chapters have already shown many ways in which the married couple and the family can grow in those elements that are linked with being Church. In the remaining portion of this chapter, I would like to reflect on several further ways for the family to become more fully Church: sharing their prayers, their decision-making, their special celebrations and their family fun.

Family Prayer

Nurturing faith is an indispensable dimension both of becoming Church and of growing as a Christian family. One of the most significant ways of nourishing faith is by sharing prayer.

Sharing prayer means more than merely reciting prayers as we kneel side by side. It is possible to recite prayers in unison without revealing any insights or concerns. It is therefore important that family members put a lot of emphasis on praying in their own words. In this way they share something of their religious faith and their spiritual life. This provides another avenue for building the family bond.

One place to share prayer is at table. The following suggestions will serve a family's prayer:

1) Family members can be encouraged to make up the grace in their own words. Usually this is spontaneous. Occasionally a

child may wish to write an original prayer ahead of time. While the traditional grace ("Bless us, O Lord, and these thy gifts...") has its merits, it can become a routine mouthing of words. A brief Scripture reading can occasionally be used, as long as it does not become a substitute for spontaneous prayer.

2) Each member of the family can take a turn in leading grace, rotating the responsibility through the week. Even a two-year-old can learn to do this (and some do it quite well). Young children pick up the knack from parents and older siblings. Any other person at table can add a prayer if desired. This can usually be done within a minute or two.

3) The prayer takes place before anyone begins to eat.

4) Holding hands during grace adds a unifying touch.

5) The prayer should usually contain a few basic elements: thanksgiving for some specific gifts; mention of some specific needs of the family and friends; a prayer for the needy, the hungry, the homeless.

6) Prayer at the family meal can also be tied in with the liturgical seasons. Placing the Advent wreath in the middle of the table and lighting the candles during grace allows the meal to become an integral part of the family's preparation for Christmas. During Lent families can place in the middle of the table a box or jar for contributions for the poor. When the meal prayer is finished family members can deposit money from their own sacrifice. Grace at Christmastime and during the Easter season can be directly related to those feasts.

The kind of prayer before meals described above serves a fourfold purpose: It teaches children how to pray. It deepens the family's faith life. It enhances the bonding power of the family meal. And it helps raise our consciousness about our responsibility to the deprived in the midst of our own abundance.

A second opportunity for family prayer occurs at bedtime. When children are very young, the whole family can gather for a brief period of prayer in which each child gets to pray in her or his own words. Some families may also wish to recite some formal prayer together.

As children get older and bedtimes differ, some families may find that nightly family prayer is difficult to maintain. That practice might give way to a parent praying with an individual child when they say goodnight.

A third way to encourage family prayer, especially when children reach their preteens and teens, is to gather together once a week for about 10 to 15 minutes. This could be done as part of a weekly family meeting (which will be discussed in the next section) or could be established as a separate event.

Here is one approach to such a weekly session: A family member begins with an opening prayer that sets the tone for the session. Another family member reads a passage from Scripture that she or he has selected and prepared beforehand. This is followed by a brief period of silent reflection. Each person is then invited to share some meaning perceived in the passage. The sharing can end with family members offering their own spontaneous prayer.

Variations can be introduced into some of the sessions: a dramatization of a biblical story or a choral reading of a Scripture text, for example. Singing or listening to a recording of a religious musical piece might sometimes add to the prayerful spirit.

It seems best to set a day of the week and time for this sharing. An alternate time can be established when necessary.

Family Meetings

Family meetings can be an important means for achieving better communication and greater intimacy. Some families schedule them on a regular basis, whether once a week, every other week or once a month. Other families hold them only when it is necessary to address certain situations. Some families prepare a carefully planned agenda and follow strict rules of order. Others have an informal gathering.

These meetings can be a separate entity, distinct from other family activities, or they can be combined with family prayer and with family fun. One family we know sets aside approximately an hour one night each week. The meeting begins with about 15 minutes of shared prayer. They then spend whatever time is necessary to air any complaints or offer suggestions about what is going on in the family. Decisions that affect the whole family are discussed and each member given an opportunity to provide input. They conclude their session by playing a game together.

There is no *best* way to incorporate meetings into the family structure. Whatever way is chosen will be beneficial for fostering communication and strengthening a healthy sense of belonging if certain ground rules are followed:

1) The entire family helps to decide the time for family meeting, the format to be followed and the matters to be discussed.

2) All family members are encouraged to attend the regularly scheduled meeting. If this is impossible on a given occasion, the meeting can be rescheduled.

3) Each person is expected to listen respectfully to what others are saying. Interruptions are not allowed.

4) No one person is permitted to dominate the discussion. Each one is given equal opportunity to speak.

5) One family member is designated to chair the meeting. It might be good to rotate this role. The chairperson's task is to see that the ground rules are followed, that the meeting moves smoothly and that the discussion stays on the topic.

What kinds of topics are discussed at family meetings? The first answer is *any* topic that a family member feels needs to be discussed. Beyond that, three areas can be addressed:

1) *Household conduct.* Air complaints that certain agreements are not being kept or enforced (household chores, times for meals, curfews). Or entertain suggestions about changing some rules and regulations.

2) *Suggestions for bettering the living situation.* "Let's spend more time together." "Perhaps the menus could be varied more." "Can we get rid of that ugly lamp in the living room and buy a new one?"

3) *Plans and decisions.* "Should I take this new job? What effect would this have on all of us?"

Regular family meetings can bring many benefits. They provide an opportunity for both children and parents to express their feelings, share ideas and participate in the running of the household. They draw the family closer together and foster better communication. One couple reported, "Ever since we started having family meetings, we find we spend more time at meals just talking to one another." Another couple observed, "The formal discussions at the family meetings have spilled over to other occasions. Now we discuss a number of family matters at a variety of times."

Another important benefit of regular meetings is that it helps the children—as well as the adults—develop skills. They learn to speak up, to listen and to disagree agreeably. Taking a turn at chairing the meeting fosters leadership ability. Participating in family decisions strengthens a child's sense of responsibility.

Family Celebrations

Families, like churches, need to gather on special occasions to celebrate. In this way they enhance their identity and build their spirit of community. Here are just a few occasions for the family to celebrate:

1) *Birthdays*. These always provide an occasion to focus special attention on individual family members. This can be done in a variety of ways. In one family we know, the parents take the birthday child to dinner alone; they have the birthday party with the whole family when they return home. In another family the entire family goes out together.

Still another variation: In a family with three daughters and two sons, the mother takes a birthday boy to lunch; the father does the same for the girls. The whole family celebrates at dinner. The birthday person selects the menu (within reason) and eats from a plate that reads, "You are special today."

Certain decorations become a part of family celebration. One family has an electric "Happy Birthday" sign that they place on the buffet. Another family includes streamers, flowers and personalized balloons. Whatever the details of birthday celebrations, the important thing is to develop a certain family tradition to celebrate the birth and the life of each family member. Such family rituals bring members closer together and affirm the value and importance of each individual.

2) *Halloween.* Some people are opposed in principle to Halloween. They claim that the practice of trick-or-treating teaches children how to be extortionists. Or they object to the "pagan" emphasis on ghosts and witches.

Halloween can obviously get out of hand, but with parental supervision the hazards and abuses can be avoided. Celebrating the Eve of All Saints can further afford a memorable opportunity for family togetherness.

The first thing on the minds of small (and not-so-small) children when they go trick-or-treating is the *treat.* In most cases *trick* doesn't enter their consciousness. Children can be taught to receive the treat graciously and say thank you. Permitting children to go only to the houses of familiar neighbors avoids the danger of becoming the victim of a crackpot. Adults can give healthy treats, money or the better types of candies and avoid distributing the worst forms of junk food.

But trick-or-treating is not the only way of celebrating Halloween. Why not also have a family Halloween party, with or without costumes? All it takes is some decorations, proper lighting, cider and donuts, and apples in a tub of water. (Inserting into the apples foil-wrapped coins of various value adds to the excitement.)

3) *Thanksgiving.* This nonreligious holiday has rich possibilities for nourishing the family's faith life as well as their love. If the family prays together on a regular basis, then the grace before meals and the family prayer during Thanksgiving week can center on some of the gifts for which persons in the household are most grateful. It is very important during this week not only to thank God, but also to thank each other. Incorporating gratitude into the family prayer is one way to do this. Another is to set aside some time at the family meeting or at dinner for family

members to tell the three things they most appreciate about one another.

Getting into the mood of giving thanks in the days before the Thursday holiday helps ensure that Thanksgiving dinner will really be a celebration of all the good things that God has bestowed upon us through one another. Inviting relatives or friends to share the day is another important way of showing gratitude; it also enhances the celebration and deepens the family's spirit of love. Expressing our gratitude on this day can inspire us to show our appreciation for each other in countless ways throughout the rest of the year.

4) *Christmas*. At Christmas we celebrate a birth, the gift of a person—God's self-giving in and through the gift of Jesus Christ. Frantic buying sprees miss the point of the feast, doing little or nothing to foster family intimacy. Christmas means caring, taking time to be together, healing loneliness and making people feel special.

There are a number of fun ways in which members of a family can share with each other in the weeks before Christmas. One family made a banner with a cloth Christmas tree on it. Under the tree are pockets numbered 1 through 24, each containing a cloth decoration. Beginning on December 1, a child attaches the decoration for the day to the cloth Christmas tree while the family sings a carol.

Another version of the same idea is to make a calendar with pockets and insert a brief seasonal Scripture reading in each pocket. The text for that day then becomes part of the meal prayer.

A family Kris Kringle exchange is another special means of sharing. Early in December, family members' names are placed in a container. Each person picks a name and becomes that person's Kris Kringle, secretly doing special things for her or him during the weeks before Christmas. These kindnesses can include anonymous notes, small treats and doing little chores. Right before Christmas the family has a Kris Kringle party at which each Kris Kringle gives a gift (within agreed-upon spending limits) and reveals his or her identity.

Families will celebrate many other occasions. Each family will weave its own traditions around Easter, the wedding anniversary, graduations and other significant situations. One family we know has a special restaurant to which they bring the children each year on the last day of school. Participation in the school play, spelling bees and championship games provide other occasions for celebration: "Win or lose, you made it. You performed well and we are proud of you!"

Family Fun

The call to be joyful is the element of being a Christian most often overlooked. Jesus spoke of his desire that "my own joy may be in you/and your joy be complete" (John 15:11). Paul picks up the same theme when he exhorts the Philippians: "Always be joyful, then, in the Lord; I repeat, be joyful" (4:4).

The adage popular a generation ago reminded us that "the family that prays together, stays together." It is at least as valid to say that "the family that plays together stays together." Taking time to enjoy each other and to have fun with one another strengthens family unity and love.

In our society many people tend to think that they are not accomplishing anything unless they are working. Play is considered wasting time or goofing off. On the contrary, play is important for human development; it has psychological, educational and social benefits. Family play is an important way members can be personally present to each other. The time they spend together in recreation shows their appreciation for each other. They are saying, in effect, "You are a person worth spending time with. It is a value for me to be with you."

The place to begin nurturing family play is within the home. Here are some ways to do that:

Play games together: ball, cards, board games, word games. Do arts, crafts and puzzles together. Encourage children to come up with creative and challenging ideas for homemade games.

Encourage family-produced entertainment. Children love to

put on skits, variety shows, contests, bazaars. They spend a lot of time preparing; then the entire family gathers for the event. Allowing for this type of fun affirms the children and nurtures development of the creative imagination.

Watch selected TV shows together as a family, and then critically analyze them. The almost total lack of Christian values in so much programming can serve as a springboard for some good discussions. Families can challenge the violence, the materialism and the sexual exploitation of women that is so much a part of television fare.

Sharing fun at home is both unifying and educational. It is an enriching and inexpensive form of entertainment which pays big dividends to all involved. But enjoying fun as a family ought not be confined to the space within four walls. There are numerous joyful yet inexpensive experiences the family can share outside the home: walking, bike rides, picnics in the park, Sunday drives, visits to the museum or planetarium. Sports events, cultural happenings and fairs also make for good family sharing.

Finally, the family can also have fun together on family vacations and visits to extended families. Sometimes you hear people praised because they "haven't taken a vacation in years." Such a statement, especially regarding a spouse and a parent, raises many questions. It is true that most of us have to make the time, put work aside and squeeze money out of the budget in order to make family vacations and visits possible. But the benefits, in terms of family bonding, joyful hearts and unforgettable memories are far more than worth the sacrifice.

If money is short, then vacations can be taken at home with plenty of built-in family events in and out of the house. Switching homes with friends for a week or so may afford a change of scene. If possible, however, family trips ought not be neglected, especially when children are in their school years. Travel is relaxing and educational—and being away from home helps parents avoid the temptation to spend the vacation doing home improvements.

Conclusion

Becoming Church is a reality that does not happen automatically. It takes place through the gathering of Christians who share common discipleship. The Christian family can appropriately be called the domestic Church to the degree that family members share their faith and love of Christ and one another in prayer, in dialogue and in the enjoyment of each other's company.

For Reflection and Discussion

1) How would you define the word *Church*? What images associated with that word are to your liking? Which do you dislike?

2) How do you feel about calling the family a domestic Church? Do you think the average Christian family experiences itself as Church?

3) What do you see as the major obstacles to family prayer? To family meetings? To family games?

4) What do you see as the principal benefits of each of the activities above?

Partner-to-Partner Inventory

1) What elements of Church do we experience in our family?
   Which are lacking?

2) Do we share prayer together? What is the nature of this
   sharing? Do we enjoy and benefit from this experience or suffer
   it merely for the sake of the partner? How would we like to see
   our shared prayer improved?

3) What form do family meetings take in our household? What is
   there about our family meetings that we find satisfactory? What
   do we find lacking? Do we have any concrete suggestions for
   making our family meetings more beneficial?

4) What traditions associated with family celebrations mean the
   most to us and to our family? How would we like to see
   celebrations enhanced in our home?

5) What do we do to have fun together? Do we spend sufficient
   time enjoying one another's company? Are we a playful family?
   Are there further ways in which we could spend more time
   playing together?

PRAYER SERVICE

The Domestic Church

Opening Prayer

Lord, you have called us to be your disciples and to gather in your name. Help us, that through our sharing as a family we may become more fully your people. We pray this in your name. Amen.

Scripture Reading

> Now the body is not a single part, but many. If a foot should say, "Because I am not a hand I do not belong to the body," it does not for this reason belong any less to the body. Or if an ear should say, "Because I am not an eye I do not belong to the body," it does not for this reason belong any less to the body. If the whole body were an eye, where would the hearing be? If the whole body were hearing, where would the sense of smell be? But as it is, God placed the parts, each one of them, in the body as he intended. If they were all one part, where would the body be? But as it is, there are many parts, yet one body....Now you are Christ's body, and individually parts of it. (1 Corinthians 12:14-20, 27, NAB)

Silent Reflection

Sharing of thoughts on the reading

Litany

This Litany reflects three different moods: thanksgiving, penitence and resolution. Couples should pause between the sections and allow themselves to settle into the mood of the prayer.

131

For enabling us to experience our family
as a Christian community,
    We thank you, Lord,

For the gift of being able to share our prayer with one another,
    We thank you, Lord.

For all of the celebrations and special occasions
that have enhanced our unity and our love,
    We thank you, Lord.

For the laughter and play we have shared together,
    We thank you, Lord.

For aspects of our behavior which are unchristian
and detrimental to forming community,
    Lord, have mercy.

For the times we have failed to share ourselves
with the rest of the family,
    Lord, have mercy.

For lack of attention and creativity at family prayer,
    Lord, have mercy.

For failure to contribute to family joy and happiness,
    Lord, have mercy.

We will strive to manifest your love and goodness more fully
in our family community,
    Lord, help us, we pray.

We will take more time to spend with each other
in meaningful ways,
    Lord, help us, we pray.

The couple add further resolutions of their own.
    Lord, help us, we pray.

132

Concluding Prayer

Refrain is recited together. The verses, taken from Psalm 111:1-8, can be recited by either spouse.

Refrain: I give thanks to Yahweh with all my heart.

I give thanks to Yahweh with all my heart,
in the meeting-place of honest people, in the assembly.
Great are the deeds of Yahweh,
to be pondered by all who delight in them.

Refrain

Full of splendor and majesty his work,
his saving justice stands firm for ever.
He gives us a memorial of his great deeds:
Yahweh is mercy and tenderness.

Refrain

He gives food to those who fear him,
he keeps his covenant ever in mind.
His works show his people his power
in giving them the birthright of the nations.

Refrain

The works of his hands are fidelity and justice,
all his precepts are trustworthy,
established for ever and ever,
accomplished in fidelity and honesty.

Refrain

Kiss of Peace

HOW BLESSED ARE the poor in spirit:
the kingdom of Heaven is theirs.
Blessed are the gentle:
they shall have the earth as inheritance.
Blessed are those who mourn:
they shall be comforted.
Blessed are those who hunger and thirst for uprightness:
they shall have their fill.
Blessed are the merciful:
they shall have mercy shown them.
Blessed are the pure in heart:
they shall see God.
Blessed are the peacemakers:
they shall be recognized as children of God.
Blessed are those who are persecuted in the cause of
    uprightness:
the kingdom of Heaven is theirs. (Matthew 5:3-10)

EIGHT

Living the Ideal in a Broken World

Throughout this book we have been reflecting on the ideals of Christian marriage. Ideals are never perfectly achieved. We pursue them seriously only with difficulty, sometimes with a gnawing doubt whether ideals work at all in a world that in many ways seems so alien to them.

Five ideals proposed in this book might be particularly difficult to achieve in contemporary life:

1) We have presented marriage as a process of growing union built on authentic personal communication. Yet we live in a world where many people fear and shun intimacy, where the pressures of "getting ahead" militate against taking the time and the risks to get close to one another.

2) Faithfulness and total commitment to a permanent relationship are essential to our notion of marriage. Yet we are immersed in a society where more and more things, from diapers to dishes, are disposable. It is an age where people, too, are disposable, especially when they stand in the way of profit. It is an age of broken relationships and of a skyrocketing divorce rate.

3) The ideal of Christian marriage as a sacrament presupposes that spouses share a life of faith. Yet, in this age of

ecumenism, marriage between persons of different religious traditions is on the rise.

4) Our view of marriage demands that the first priority be dedication and personal presence to one another, not to things. Yet as inflation and unemployment increase, we are feeling more and more the strains of financial stress.

5) We insist that no married couple exist merely for themselves and their children, but must reach out to the wider human community. This begins with the broader family of relatives and in-laws. Yet we live in a highly mobile society, and people cherish their independence. Both of these factors present problems when we determine how we are going to relate to parents, siblings and more distant relatives.

Is it possible to realize the ideals of Christian marriage in this troubled and broken world? In this chapter we look more closely at the five areas of tension described above. In doing so, we will look for further practical implications that can help us work toward the achievement of these ideals despite the obstacles.

The Need to Communicate

Our age is gifted with unprecedented technological means of communication, and yet we live in a world where nations, neighbors, relatives and spouses so often cannot get along. We thirst for greater sharing and deeper union, and yet too frequently find ourselves alone and estranged even from those closest to us, unable to break down the barriers that keep us apart.

The ability to communicate is essential for working toward the goals of Christian marriage. In several places throughout the book we have reflected upon some of the characteristics of good communication. Here we underscore three major insights that can help our efforts toward achieving such communication.

1) *Effective communication is a dialogue, not a monologue.* Dialogue takes place when a couple respect the rights of each other to speak and to respond, and when they each accept the responsibility to listen. Such communication presupposes a basic

equality in the relationship. It also presupposes that we are willing to invest the time and take the risks involved. Several principles are important to ensure that our communication is truly a dialogue:

First, neither person talks down to the other. Dialogue cannot take place when the all-wise one is instructing the ignorant one. Nor can it happen when the all-righteous person is chiding the partner perceived as always wrong, or when the spouse "in charge" is barking orders to be obeyed blindly. The dynamic in these situations reflects a denial of equality in the partnership.

Second, we need to make our statements in such a way as to allow for mature response. This means that we cannot present our remarks as the last word but, rather, as an invitation for further insights, suggestions, even disagreement. Sarcasm, name-calling, insults and put-downs close the door to such response. Without response and interchange there can be no dialogue.

Third, we must listen and hear what the other is trying to communicate. This involves being personally present to the partner, and making sure that what is said is properly understood.

Fourth, we must offer appropriate response. It is rude and insulting to allow another's words to be left hanging in midair. Ignoring what our spouse has said and acting as if nothing had been spoken blocks communication instantly.

2) *Both partners should express their feelings, not just their ideas.* They need, for example, to be able to talk about their feelings so that they can help each other understand them and channel them in a life-giving way.

In order for this kind of intimate yet difficult communication to take place, we must create an atmosphere of acceptance and trust. Every feeling that a person has is a reality that deserves respect. To deny, ridicule or make light of the feelings of another is a rejection of an important part of that person. The ability "to walk in the shoes" of another, to feel what the other feels, to be in touch with what underlies those feelings signifies a high degree of personal maturity. Such sensitivity helps create an environment that makes a constructive expression of feelings possible.

Much in American culture militates against the honest expression of feelings; such display is considered a sign of weakness to be tolerated with condescension in the female but reproved in the male. Feelings, however, are an essential part of being human. They are repressed only at great cost to our total personal development.

Honest acknowledgment and acceptance of my feelings will allow me to recognize the validity of my spouse's feelings. Having the inner freedom to speak my own feelings will make it easier for me to encourage my spouse's expression of feelings. According to the wise author of the Book of Ecclesiastes, there is:

A time for tears,
a time for laughter;
a time for mourning,
a time for dancing. (3:4)

Being able to enter fully into those diverse moments that constitute the rhythm of life is critical for the development of more intimate marital communication.

3) *Constructive criticism is an important part of communication.* "Constructive criticism" means expressing in a spirit of love an honest evaluation of the virtues and strengths, the faults and limitations that exist in oneself, in one's spouse and in the relationship. This mutual evaluation fosters growth of the best qualities in the couple and in the marriage. Unlike destructive criticism, which tears down the other person, it does not inhibit or cripple the good that is already present.

It is important that the various elements contained in this description of constructive criticism be kept in balance. Honesty must always be expressed in love. Limitations and faults must be observed against the backdrop of strengths and virtues.

Destructive criticism harps on faults. "You're as slow as molasses." "You're a slob in the kitchen." "You always keep me waiting." Constructive criticism builds on the good qualities and positive points already present and indicates room for improvement. "I appreciate the care with which you tend to your work. Do you think you could speed up a little?" "You're an excellent cook. Perhaps you could clean up more as you go along." "I know you're extremely busy. Next time could we rearrange our scheduling so I won't have to wait so long?"

In order for criticism to be effective, it is also necessary to distinguish what can be changed from what cannot or should not be changed. We can learn to turn a faucet off tightly, to chew gum less noisily, to lower our voice when people are sleeping. We might not be able to change a nasal tone or to get along on less than nine hours of sleep a night. If a person cannot look at food before noon, a daily lecture on the need for a nutritious breakfast is hardly appropriate.

Finally, we must perceive our spouse in the context of our own self-perception. "Take the log out of your own eye first, and then you will see clearly enough to take the splinter out of your brother's eye" (Matthew 7:5).

The ability to engage in constructive criticism presupposes the truthfulness and courage required to give it, the humility and understanding necessary to receive and discuss it, and a bond of mutual trust and love that enables a couple to grow through it. Constructive criticism is an art. Through such art, we build an intimate relationship.

The Rising Divorce Rate

Older adults may have a difficult time remembering a grade-school classmate whose parents were divorced. Today's seven-year-old may be able to rattle off a substantial list of playmates and school friends from broken homes. This environment of increased divorce does not leave married people untouched.

Most of us have relatives and friends who have gone through a divorce. Some marriages that we considered quite "ideal" have disintegrated. We may begin to wonder whether permanency in marriage is any longer achievable in this mixed-up world. We come to realize that there is no marriage, including our own, that is immune against the perils of breakdown and divorce.

Do we give up? Do we allow the possibility of divorce to paralyze us or to drain our efforts toward building a lasting bond? Will our fears of marital breakdown become self-fulfilling prophecies?

While we grow in awareness of the risks and perils involved in marriage and of the increased possibilities of divorce, we must also grow in our own self-determination. We must decide that we *want* to make our marriage work and then utilize all the inner and outer resources available to make a success of our relationship. We must reject the notion that what happens to our marriage will be a matter of fate or external pressures. We must believe in ourselves and the power of our love so we can do all we can *now* to build together the strongest marriage possible and to satisfy each other's deepest needs and yearnings. Our best efforts will not provide a guarantee against divorce, but we nevertheless can provide the best possible foundation for a happy outcome.

Married couples must also be mindful of their responsibility to those whose marriages have ended in divorce. There is no room for feelings of superiority or for condemnation. Rather than looking upon divorced people as failures, married couples can enter empathetically into the heartbreak and disruption that all divorce involves. They can grow in compassion and sensitivity. They can be aware of the heroic efforts many divorced people have made to keep their marriages alive.

Rather than estranging divorced people from the life of the community, married couples need to search creatively for ways to help them build their lives anew. This can be done by extending friendship, by listening, by providing special help to single parents, especially during the adjustment period. Married couples can also make a point of including the divorced in their social, Church and community gatherings.

Continued communication and interchange between married and divorced people will be mutually beneficial. Married people can learn about hazards to marriage from the divorced. The divorced need the support, guidance and companionship that the married community can provide.

Finally, in the ongoing dicussion among Catholics about the possibility of remarriage after divorce, two points need to be kept in mind:

1) The ethical and canonical discussions of this topic must find their roots in a very positive theology of marriage as a sacrament of Christ's love for his people and in a deep appreciation of the redemptive and transforming spiritual power of marriage.

2) While recent efforts to improve the annulment process are laudable, we should avoid the hazards of overusing this approach as the only solution to the divorce problem.

There are certainly a variety of circumstances that indicate some "marriages" were never real marriages. These include lack of serious consent or inability at the time to enter into an exclusive, permanent marital commitment. But our desire to help divorced people marry again in a way recognized by the Church must not lead to an abuse of the annulment process. Many marriages that are now irreparably broken were once real marriages that endured the tests of many years and brought happiness and satisfaction. It can be dishonest, insulting and ultimately a discredit to marriage and to the annulment process to pretend that such marriages never existed. It is better to face honestly the deeper question: Is it possible for a marriage that once existed to have irreversibly disintegrated to such an extent that it is no longer a true marriage?

Interfaith Marriages

Today there are more marriages between people with profound religious differences than there were a generation ago. From the Catholic perspective the reasons are obvious. The Second Vatican Council promoted a healthier attitude toward other Christian denominations and world religions and has encouraged closer association with them. This has contributed to an increase of marriages between persons of different denominations and different religions.

Also, within Catholicism a wider diversity of beliefs and ethical opinions is overtly expressed than was possible before the Council. It is therefore important to keep in mind that religious differences exist not only in interdenominational marriages, but also in marriages between persons of the same denomination.

There are five areas in which such differences can affect the achievement of a happy marriage:

1) *Commitment to Christ.* Individual Christians can seriously differ about what they actually believe in regard to Christ. Do they both accept Christ as the enfleshment of the Son of God, the Word of God? Do they agree that he is Lord and Savior of all? Do they believe that the crucified Christ is risen from the dead and continues to guide us and lead us to God?

Beyond these areas of traditional Christian belief, there can be major differences in the personal meaning that Christ has for us. Is he a mere lawgiver, a distant model from the past, a meaningless abstraction—or a personal friend who is intimately present? To what degree is Christ a central point of reference in a couple's decision-making and in their perception of each other and their marriage?

What does it mean for each of us to be followers of Christ? For one spouse it might mean merely abiding by the Ten Commandments and the laws of the Church. For the other it may involve a dedicated pursuit of the ideals of the Sermon on the Mount and a radical openness to the Spirit given us by the crucified and risen Christ.

2) *Commitment to Church affiliation.* "Belonging to the Church" can mean anything from nominal membership due to past Baptism to attendance at Christmas and Easter to an explicit involvement in the life and mission of the Church that is a significant part of one's life. Special tensions can arise in a marriage where there are profound differences in the way spouses relate to the Church.

3) *The meaning of Scripture.* There are two aspects to this issue. First, what role does Scripture have in the shaping of one's

142

faith consciousness and one's spirituality? Is it a regular part of one's reading and one's prayer, or does Scripture have very little practical impact on one's faith life?

The second aspect has to do with the interpretation of Scripture. A person who insists on a fundamentalist or literalist interpretation of Scripture will have an understanding of the Bible that is very different from one who interprets Scripture in light of its historical, cultural and literary context. In recent years some Christian denominations have split over these two approaches to the interpretation of Scripture; it is not surprising that such a difference could cause serious, perhaps unresolvable difficulties in a marriage.

4) *Beliefs about marriage.* Notable differences also arise in the degree of religious meaning individuals find in marriage. On the level of moral convictions, the differences can be drastic and fraught with tension. How compatible are a couple's views regarding the morality of abortion, contraception, sterilization, extramarital affairs, diverse sexual actions in the marriage?

5) *Religious formation of children.* In interdenominational marriages, the first question concerns the denomination in which the child will be reared. Where there are differences within the same denomination, another set of questions surfaces. Will we have the child baptized in infancy or allow the child to decide at a later age? Will we insist that the child go to church with the parent who attends weekly, or allow the child to stay home with the parent who never attends? Will we raise the child in the strict tradition or in a more liberal approach?

It is more important that two people contemplating marriage deal with the issues in these five areas in a forthright manner prior to the wedding. They must identify where they both stand in regard to these matters. They must also determine whether they can in fact resolve their religious differences, or whether their divergent views present an insurmountable obstacle to a happy marriage. It is a mistake to pretend that the problem will automatically resolve itself after the marriage.

Even when agreements have been made prior to the

marriage, the couple must continue to share with each other how they feel about the dissimilarities in their religious views, and about the way these divergences actually affect their marriage. They must be willing to evaluate the efforts they are making in working out their religious differences in a manner compatible to the growth of their marriage.

Most of all, such a couple must strive to explore the ways in which they can share the elements of faith they do hold in common through discussion, shared prayer and cooperative participation in worthy human causes. Very often what binds us together in the area of religion outweighs what separates us.

Financial Stress

We may have lofty ideals about how important it is to trust each other, to be generous, to put spiritual values before material ones. When we face the realities of money and hard financial decisions, however, our ideals are seriously put to the test.

There are two reasons why money can be so problematic in a marriage. First, money is often a key to power; the question of who owns and who controls the money in a marriage is a significant one. Second, even the healthiest of relationships can be strained by financial difficulties and by the struggle to keep a budget balanced in the midst of rising costs and the growing desire for affluence.

In financial matters, the couple's *attitude* toward money is of paramount importance. If they agree on the general approach to four basic issues, most of the financial difficulties can be worked out in harmony.

1) *Ownership of the money.* Does the "breadwinner" claim ownership of the money and then dole it out condescendingly to the spouse who has little or no outside source of income? If both work, does each make separate claim to the portion earned? Or are both co-owners of whatever money comes in?

In a marriage between two responsible people, salaried money must be considered earned by both. This is especially true when one spouse is working full-time without pay, keeping the home and taking care of the children, so that the other spouse is free to engage in an outside job.

2) *Management of money.* Who budgets, keeps the books and writes the checks? Again, where both spouses are responsible people, both must share decisions about how money is divided and spent. The assignment of financial tasks should be done according to mutual choice and competence, not according to stereotyped sex roles. Regardless of which spouse performs these tasks, both need to be fully informed.

3) *Establishing priorities.* In practice, are people more important than things? Is the well-being of persons in the family really served by making more money, saving money or accumulating possessions?

The gospel's clear answer is, of course, in favor of persons. If a couple is in agreement on this matter, many problems can be avoided. Placing persons over things will balance the amount of time and energy spent making money against the amount spent building relationships with each other and with the children. It will also influence how money is spent and keep the proper emphasis on shared pleasures and activities, on opportunities for personal enrichment and the development of talents.

4) *Giving to people, causes and organizations outside the family unit.* The family has responsibilities beyond its own boundaries. It has a need to share with others its time, talents and material goods. A couple must make decisions to donate time and energy with mutual agreement and without detriment to their primary family responsibilities.

The Extended Family

When we get married we set out on a new way of life. We are now on our own. We must make our own decisions and be responsible for the building of our own family. This is an endeavor which absorbs our attention and energy. We realize that what happens to our marriage rests ultimately on our shoulders, and on no one else's.

How do we integrate these dramatic changes in our life with our need to be in touch with our roots, with our ongoing responsibility to the relationships we have built up over the course of our lives? How do we face the fact that marriage immediately involves us in a new relationship and accompanying responsibilities to our spouse's family? In facing these questions four observations are helpful:

1) *We need to integrate two realities in our marriage.* Our own marriage must become the primary relationship in our life; at the same time, we continue to bear responsibility toward our parents and relatives. We need to avoid the extreme of relying so much on our parents that we relegate our spouse to secondary importance in major decisions, and the opposite extreme of so shutting our parents out of our lives that we resist any advice they have to offer.

We can show respect to our parents for the experience and wisdom they possess, even while realizing that we are the ones who must make the decisions that affect our marriage. This can be done by keeping in communication with our parents and by seeking their advice especially in their areas of expertise. We can also be sensitive to them in those matters that will especially affect them—a move across the country, for instance.

2) *Our marriage marks a significant passage in our parents' lives.* Our "leaving home" may call for a difficult adjustment on their part. Our marriage introduces a new element into our relationships with them; we too are married adults, peers instead of children. They can no longer relate to us in the same way; in a sense they "lose" us. They know we no longer "need" them as we once did. Therefore, as we work toward building a new relationship with our parents, we need to discover ways in which they can continue to make an important contribution to us and to our children.

3) *We must respect and be sensitive to our spouse's family.* We can put jealousy aside to encourage and support the building up of these relationships. We can provide opportunities for our

spouse to be with parents and relatives.

4) *Those who are dear to our spouse take on special meaning for us.* We therefore need to make an authentic effort to form a personal bond of friendship with our in-laws.

Conclusion

The Christian vision of marriage is sorely tested by the tensions and stresses of today's world. These obstacles, however, need not conquer us. With mutual determination, communication and goodwill, we can continue to make progress toward achieving our highest ideals.

For Reflection or Discussion

1) The author cites five areas of tension surrounding marriage. Which of these do you perceive as the greatest hazard to marital happiness? Are there other tensions you would add? Why?

2) Which of the three aspects of communication cited by the author do you find most difficult? How can you overcome the difficulty?

3) Has divorce ever touched you personally? How did you respond to marital breakup, your own or someone else's? Has your experience changed the way you might respond to divorce in the future?

4) Probe the extent to which you share faith with those close to you, regardless of denominational differences. Where do the deepest differences lie? How can you reach across them?

5) What are your views on the ownership and management of money in a marriage? What spending priorities would you place first?

Partner-to-Partner Inventory

1) To what degree does our communication contain these elements of true dialogue: respecting each other's dignity, rather than talking down; making statements in a way that invites response, even if this includes disagreement; listening to what the other is saying and trying to grasp the meaning of what is being said; responding to each other in an appropriate way?

2) Do we express our feelings to one another? Do we create an atmosphere of understanding and sympathy that invites our partner to be expressive of what she or he feels?

3) Are we as willing to accept criticism from our partner as we are to give it? In what ways do we criticize constructively? What elements of destructiveness are contained in the way we criticize?

4) What are the principal areas of common religious faith? What are the main differences in our religious beliefs and practices? Do these differences cause any difficulty in our relationship? If they do, what steps are we taking to resolve them?

5) What major agreements and disagreements do we have in regard to: the place money has on our scale of priorities; our attitudes toward ownership; the way we budget and manage our money?

6) On a scale of one to 10, how do we assess the way each of us gets along with our blood relatives and with our in-laws? What specific reasons support our assessment? In what ways do we need to improve these relationships?

Toward the Ideal

Opening Prayer

Lord Jesus, during your journey on this earth you showed us how to relate to others with kindness, compassion and love. Help us to relate to one another and to our families and friends with similar sensitivity and concern. We pray this, Lord, in your name. Amen.

Scripture Reading

Be compassionate just as your Father is compassionate. Do not judge, and you will not be judged; do not condemn, and you will not be condemned; forgive, and you will be forgiven. Give, and there will be gifts for you: a full measure, pressed down, shaken together, and overflowing, will be poured into your lap; because the standard you use will be the standard used for you.

(Luke 6:36-38)

Silent reflection

Sharing of thoughts on the reading

Litany

This Litany reflects three different moods: thanksgiving, penitence and resolution. Couples should pause between the sections and allow themselves to settle into the mood of the prayer.

For the quality of communication we have already achieved in our marriage,
> We thank you, Lord.

For the gift of our families,
   We thank you, Lord.

For our faith, and our ability to share it with one another,
   We thank you, Lord.

For the material gifts you provide for us,
   We thank you, Lord.

For any offense we have given to one another
in the way we converse,
   Lord, have mercy.

For the times in which we have failed in charity
toward our relatives,
   Lord, have mercy.

For the ways in which we have lacked faith,
or been reluctant to share faith,
   Lord, have mercy.

For ever allowing financial considerations
to stand in the way of our growth in intimacy,
   Lord, have mercy.

We will continue to give priority
to improving the quality of our communication,
   Lord, help us, we pray.

We will strive to build on what is already good
in our relationship with our families,
and work together to address the difficulties,
   Lord, help us, we pray.

We resolve to find ways of more deeply sharing our faith
with one another,
   Lord, help us, we pray.

We will strive toward an ever more Christian use of money,
   Lord, help us, we pray.

The couple add further resolutions of their own.
    Lord, help us, we pray.

Concluding Prayer

This, then, is what I pray, kneeling before the Father, from whom every fatherhood, in heaven or on earth, takes its name. In the abundance of his glory may he, through his Spirit, enable you to grow firm in power with regard to your inner self, so that Christ may live in your hearts through faith, and then, planted in love and built on love, with all God's holy people you will have the strength to grasp the breadth and the length, the height and the depth; so that, knowing the love of Christ, which is beyond knowledge, you may be filled with the utter fullness of God.

Glory be to him whose power, working in us, can do infinitely more than we can ask or imagine; glory be to him from generation to generation in the Church and in Christ Jesus for ever and ever. Amen. (Ephesians 3:14-21)

Kiss of Peace

Conclusion

*I*n contrast to the prophets of doom we have focused, from a Christian perspective, on the promise of marriage, on what offers hope for our married lives, what challenges us to reach beyond our present limitations and strive for a richer, more rewarding marital experience.

We are hopeful because God has created humans as sexual beings. God wills that we grow in personal union. This union is meant to be expressed in a unique way in marriage.

We are hopeful because Christ is the Word of God enfleshed and has united us with God and with one another in a new way. The ongoing presence of the crucified and risen Christ inspires and enables married couples to manifest Christ's love in their own relationship. In this way we minister to each other and to the wider community; we promote in the world today the reign of God proclaimed by Jesus Christ. By undergoing the many deaths involved in marriage with faith, trust and love, we grow toward a more life-giving relationship with each other. Christ's ongoing self-gift in bread and wine provides insight into the meaning of our shared meals and the sexual expression of our love.

The foundations of our hope bring a corresponding

challenge. The transformation of marriage which Christ makes possible does not take place automatically. We must freely respond to the challenge of believing in ourselves and in the power of unselfish love. We must be willing to die to the fears, anxieties and self-centeredness that hold us back, so that we can become increasingly free to commit ourselves to a life of faithfulness, personal concern and generosity with one another.

There are abundant reasons for hope. May the power of that hope inspire renewed commitment to meet the challenge of marriage today!